William Porter

Alcohol Explained

For my wife.

Contents

3

1. Introduction

Most riddles we face in life are like jigsaw puzzles with missing pieces. We try to put together the pieces we have as best we can, then we guess at the missing pieces to try to understand the overall picture. With alcohol consumption and alcoholism we almost have the opposite problem. We have too many pieces. It's like a puzzle of a hundred pieces, but when you open the box you find there are ten thousand pieces in there. There is so much information out there on alcohol, alcoholism and addiction, but what are the key factors that we need to grasp in order to understand why so many people drink, and why some find it so difficult to stop?

In fact it gets even more complicated than that because some of those hundred pieces we need aren't even in the box, but are in other boxes for other puzzles.

Alcohol consumption and alcoholism is made up of the chemical, physical, physiological, and psychological effects that alcohol has on human beings, and the accumulative impact of these effects. I myself spent 25 years of my life drinking, however I have always been curious and have always sought practical answers to understand anything that takes my interest. Throughout my drinking life (and even since I have stopped drinking) I would research and seek to understand any particular aspects of the effects of alcohol that became apparent to me. So when I was in my early twenties and found that on the nights I drank I would wake up in the middle of the night and be unable to get back to sleep, I researched the impact alcohol has on sleep. Over the years I continued to think about and to analyse my drinking. I had no thoughts of writing about the subject, I just took an interest in it and looked to understand it, and as alcohol took more and more of a grip on me, so I spent more and more time trying to understand it. I did this using my own research and by analysing my personal experiences.

As things became increasingly desperate I turned to Alcoholics Anonymous thinking it would serve to further my understanding. Unfortunately it didn't. Alcoholics Anonymous is essentially a spiritual programme. It is based on the premise that God will provide the solution. This is fine if you are looking for a spiritual answer, but I wasn't. I wanted a logical and scientific answer. If God, in whatever shape or form he or she may exist, allows innocent children to die painful and degrading deaths, why on earth should he save me, a middle-aged city lawyer, from his own greed for alcohol? I am not debating the existence of God; I just struggled to understand why he or she would get so directly involved in this area and not others. If God does exist then it seems to me that rather than solve our problems for us, he or she instead provides us with the potential for great intelligence, understanding, wisdom, and compassion. It is then left up to us to use these to solve our own problems.

What I could never accept, from the very beginning, was that there is an irrational, collective insanity that is alcoholism; that it is impossible to provide some form of rationalisation for it, on whatever level; that it is impossible to understand the reasons that the alcoholic reaches for each and every drink. Some people think that they just become obsessed with things, and that alcohol just happens to be the object of their obsession. But if this is the case, why aren't there a similar number of people obsessed with drinking water or juice? There are an estimated 17.6 million people in the US alone with alcohol dependency. Why isn't there a similar number of people drinking too much water? You may think it is because drinking too much water isn't bad for you. In fact it is, hyponatremia is a condition caused by drinking too much water and it can be fatal. Why is it alcohol specifically that so many people seem to become obsessed with?

One thing that became apparent to me from listening to drinkers, both those with a problem and 'normal' drinkers, was that I wasn't unique in wanting to understand the phenomenon, and more importantly I began to realise that the knowledge and understanding I had could help others. This is why Alcohol Explained exists. Its purpose is to provide an understanding of alcohol consumption, alcoholism and addiction generally, and to provide a practical solution for those wanting to quit. It is my conclusions based on my research and my observations of my own drinking.

For those who are reading this book out of interest there is no reason to read further in this chapter; you can proceed straight to Chapter 2. However, for those who are intending to stop drinking, for those who consider they may have a problem, or for those who are considering the possibility of either stopping or cutting down with the help of this book, there are a few tips worth giving at this stage so as to ensure you get the best you can out of this book.

Firstly, if you are still drinking there is no need to stop before reading this book. There are some caveats to this. The key to this book is the information it provides. It will only be of benefit to you if you can understand and absorb this information. If you have drunk alcohol before you actually start reading on any particular day, you will impair your ability to understand and absorb the information contained here. The more you have drunk, the more this ability will be impaired. It is best if you can read it each day before you start drinking. However, equally, if you are a chronic alcoholic you are unlikely to be able to read, understand, and absorb the information in this book while suffering from severe alcohol withdrawal. If you are in this position, the best way to overcome this problem is to just concentrate on one chapter a day. Read this one chapter as often as you can during the day. The chapters are fairly short and concise and you will be able, over the course of a day, to absorb (through sheer repetition if nothing else) enough to understand the information contained in these pages.

Secondly, if you are drinking while reading this book, the most effective method of stopping is to ensure that when you do drink you do so in a quiet and private environment if at all possible. You should be checking out everything I say with reference to your own drinking. You need to do as I did and I start analysing and thinking about your drinking while you are doing it, concentrating on the taste and effect of each drink, the accumulated effect of many drinks, and the physical effect as these drinks start to wear off. Ultimately, this book is just a collection of words, it's just a bunch of ideas. These ideas will only be of help to you if you can prove to yourself that they are the truth. The best way of doing this is with reference to your own drinking. So when you drink, you need to do so somewhere quiet and private so you can really concentrate on the entire experience and apply what you have read to your own drinking.

Finally, you should note that drinking while you are reading this book only applies if you are still drinking. If you have stopped, no matter how short a period you have stopped for, there is no need to start drinking again before reading this book. You can still test what I am saying with reference to your own memory and by applying your own common sense and logic.

2.   The Physiological Effects of Drinking

Alcohol is an anaesthetic and a depressant. This is an accepted medical fact. If we are feeling tired or in pain it will take the edge off this. However, it is also a fact that the human body and mind is not a passive object; it is reactive, and will react to the world around it and to the food and drugs we put into it. The brain has its own store of drugs that it releases into our bloodstream as and when they are required. It will release these in times of stress, hunger, and fear, and will also release them in reaction to external drugs that enter our system. If we regularly take a drug then our brain and body will react to this, and will even act in expectation of this. Indeed, the more often we take an external drug, the more proficient our body will become in countering its effects.

To give an example, I drink coffee. I drink a fairly good amount of it in the morning, then I tend not to have any in the afternoons and evenings. When I wake up in the morning I tend to feel very groggy until I have had my first coffee. But before I drank coffee I wasn't groggy all the time because I hadn't had coffee, and I felt much as I do now after I have had a coffee; that is to say, pretty bright and breezy. This all makes perfectly good common sense. As a child (and even as an adult when I did not regularly imbibe caffeine), when I woke up my brain released stimulants into my system and I

11

felt awake and ready to start the day. Then at some point I tried coffee. Coffee contains caffeine, which is a stimulant, the effect of which is that I immediately felt more awake. So I started having a morning coffee on a regular basis. However, my brain realised that an alien stimulant was being put into me in the morning, so it stopped releasing its own stimulant. Without my morning hit of caffeine I feel groggy and disorientated, and when I have had my caffeine I feel pretty much as I ought to. I also know from giving up caffeine that the body also responds when the caffeine is withdrawn. The groggy feeling gets less and less until it is entirely gone within four to five days. All that is happening is that my body compensates again for the lack of external stimulant and goes back to providing its own stimulant. This experience is something the vast majority of people can relate to. So if we accept that the body acts in this way in relation to a stimulant, why would it not react in a similar, if opposite, way to a depressant?

To put the point another way, everyone knows that the more we drink, the more we build up a tolerance to the alcohol and the more we are capable of drinking. Richard Burton was drinking three to four bottles of spirits a day at one stage. Most people don't even drink that much water in a day! Richard Burton was obviously a physically very strong man to be able to cope with that amount of alcohol in a day, but even he must have built up to that level of drinking over time. Even the strongest person on the planet couldn't sit down and drink four bottles of spirits in a day, having never imbibed a drop of alcohol before, and expect to survive.

If you look at how much you could comfortably handle when you first started drinking compared with the amount you could drink after a few years, I am sure you will see a marked increase. This is pretty standard stuff and in no way controversial, and the same applies to many other things such as smoking, caffeine intake, etc. But how many of us have stopped to consider what has actually changed that allows us to imbibe a larger amount of a particular poison, an amount that would have left us extremely ill or even dead had we imbibed it in the first instance? It is not, for example, that our liver becomes stronger. The liver is not a muscle that when exercised becomes stronger. In fact, the more we pummel it the weaker it gets. So what does change?

The changes are in fact twofold. Firstly, those parts of our brain and nervous system that are particularly vulnerable to the depressive effects of alcohol become more sensitive so that they can work even when under the influence of the anaesthetising effects of alcohol. Secondly, the body becomes more proficient at manufacturing and releasing stimulants and stress hormones to counteract the effect of the alcohol. This is a perfectly natural and healthy reaction. It is the human body dealing with and countering the poisonous effects of an external substance so that we can survive it. The stronger and healthier the human, the more proficiently their body will counter the poisonous effects of the alcohol in this way.

It is also the case that the more often we imbibe alcohol and the greater the quantity we imbibe, the better and more efficient our bodies become over time in countering it. However, perfectly natural and healthy though it may be, the fact of the matter is that when we have parts of our brain and nervous system that are more sensitive, and when we have an increased amount of stimulants and stress hormones in our system, we feel not just unrelaxed but usually out-and-out nervous and anxious. The more we drink, the more pronounced this feeling of nervousness and worry is when the alcohol wears off, and it is quite usual for it to cause full-blown depression. After all, the alcohol will wear off, but the nervous feeling caused by the increased sensitivity and stimulants will remain for some time after.

There are numerous studies dealing with these two effects; however, for practical purposes, the science behind this is neither here nor there. All we need to know is that the relaxing effect of a drink is soon replaced by a corresponding feeling of anxiety. One drink will produce a relatively minor feeling of relaxation and a correspondingly minor feeling of anxiety. However, if we consume larger quantities then the feeling of anxiety is correspondingly increased and can evolve from anxiety into out-and-out depression. It is also the case that over time the effects become more pronounced as the body becomes more proficient in countering the effects of the alcohol. There is in fact a very clear connection between depression and alcohol, and self-harm and suicide are much more common in people with alcohol problems. Indeed, alcoholism is a factor in about 30% of all completed suicides and approximately 7% of those with alcohol dependence will die by suicide. In the US drunk tanks they constantly have a guard on suicide watch because inmates with hangovers are so much more likely to attempt suicide.

No doubt some people will claim that those with a mental illness are more prone to problem drink and are also more prone to depression. That may or may not be the case, but the simple fact is that hangovers cause depression whether you are mentally ill or not. Even for those with mental health issues, the withdrawal from alcohol will only make things worse. No matter how bad you think you are, you will be much worse off if you are drinking.

Drinker's remorse is a very common hangover symptom. It is usually assumed that this is due to things that the person has done when they were inebriated that they then regret the following day. This may exacerbate the problem, but the real cause of it is the chemical imbalance in the brain and body. This is why people often feel depressed the day after drinking, and when we are depressed we naturally focus on the most negative parts of our lives, whatever they may be, even if these are otherwise minor things that would ordinarily cause us little or no consternation at all. Of course, when we spend time concentrating on the worst, most negative parts of our lives, the more miserable we become, and if we are depressed anyway due to the chemical imbalance in our brains then we are more likely to view these negative things as overpowering and awful, and thus the tendency is to just spiral down.

This is why there is this tendency to look at things such as anger, guilt, and regret when trying to answer the question of why people develop a drinking problem. When someone is depressed as a result of drinking they are not depressed because of an actual reason, they are depressed because of the direct chemical reaction to the previous drinking. However, this depression causes them to dwell on anything and everything they can in their life that is negative. The hung-over mind will always find the most disturbing thing in any panorama and focus in on it. This is essentially what the chemically depressed drinker does with their life. Every single human being on the planet has any number of negative things in their lives they can dwell on if they want to, or if they are depressed due to a chemical imbalance in their brains (be it caused by drinking or anything else).

However, when the depression is caused by a chemical imbalance which in itself is caused by the previous drinking, it can be relieved by more drink. Imagine the brain working normally. We then introduce a depressant (alcohol). The brain cannot therefore work normally, so part of it becomes more sensitive so it can work while still under the influence of the depressant. It also releases stimulants and stress hormones to counter the depressant. The alcohol is then removed but the stimulants remain, and we are left feeling nervous, anxious, out of sorts, and even out-and-out depressed. But if we then imbibe more alcohol we immediately get rid of the nervous, anxious, depressed feeling.

In essence, the depression derives from the fact that the brain has been reset to work when under the influence of alcohol, so without the alcohol the brain is on hyper drive. Therefore, if our depressed drinker takes a drink, the brain then gets back to being on a nearer to normal level and, surprise surprise, he or she feels much better and the negative things they have been focusing on in their alcohol-withdrawn depression suddenly cease to worry them, or at least worry them a lot less. So they genuinely believe that there are certain parts of their life that cause them misery and depression and that drinking relieves this depression. In fact it does, but what they miss is that it is the drinking that has caused the depression in the first place. The depression isn't just caused by the chemical imbalance resulting from the previous drinks, it is also exacerbated by the physical side effects such as lack of sleep (which is dealt with in detail in a later chapter) and nausea, and the physical degradation generally. These all contribute to our depressed state. So we either suffer the ill effects, the mental anguish, and the depression until it wears off, or we drink again. If we drink again the alcohol depresses the physical side effects, so we immediately feel better. However, when that alcohol wears off, the depression and anxiety return.

This is one of the key strands to understanding alcohol. It relieves the depression and anxiety caused by the effects of the previous drinks. The drinker in question can be as successful, as lucky, as rich, as famous, or as powerful as it is possible for a person to be. It does not matter who a human being is or what they have. They can be the luckiest, most successful person in the world. But if they have had a right old skinful the night before, they will wake up feeling depressed, and only another drink will take away that depression.

18

Alcoholism and problem drinking often seems illogical to those on the outside; indeed, it is often equally perplexing for the alcoholic or problem drinker themselves. However, there is nothing illogical in this. Would you rather have everything and be depressed, and by depressed I mean properly, chronically depressed? Or would you rather have nothing and be happy? This is the choice the alcoholic faces. No matter what they have, the chemical effect of the alcohol causes them to be depressed and miserable. And only a drink will relieve this. Even if you think you would opt for having everything and be depressed, how long do you think you would last if there was one thing you could do to relieve your depression, and that thing was freely available and was offered to you several times a day, and everyone else around you was imbibing it happily?

This is why alcohol can have such a strong hold on people, causing them to sacrifice their friends, family, job, home, even their very life. Often with famous and successful people who are alcoholic, people look at them and wonder why, for someone who seems to have everything, they are so unhappy and turn to drinking. In fact, they are simply doing what everyone else does. They drink because it makes them feel good, but over time the drink itself causes them to be unhappy. However, they cannot see this because it is also the drink that seems to relieve their unhappiness, so they keep drinking and exacerbate the problem. Rich and successful people are just as likely to take a drink as anyone else; in fact, they are often more likely to drink and to drink too much. For most people, their drinking is tempered by the fact that they have to go to work, or it is constrained by finances. For famous people such as film stars and musicians, not only do they have more free time on their hands, they also spend much more time socialising where alcoholic drinks are served, they have more money to spend on drink, they can often work while under the influence of alcohol, and so they are simply more likely, or more able, to drink irresponsibly and end up with alcohol problems.

This is why so many alcoholics believe they are a breed apart; they are not happy no matter what they have in life, and the only thing that can truly take away their misery is a drink. No matter what they have in life and no matter how happy they ought to be, they will be depressed because of the chemical imbalance caused by the drink. And they believe that this depression can only be relieved by more drink. This is of course correct, but the crucial part that they are missing is that it is the alcohol that has caused them to be depressed in the first place and that relieving this depression by drinking is partial and temporary. The only permanent and complete cure is for them to stop drinking. The irony is that problem drinkers often spend thousands of pounds on expensive counselling to work out why they are so unhappy so they can in turn stop drinking, but in fact they need to go about things in exactly the opposite way: stop drinking, allow the effects to wear off, then take stock of their lives. They will find that the things they were getting depressed about when they were drinking either cease to worry them or at least become much more manageable and less overpowering.

Really, what more powerful factor could you need to create a chronic addiction than a substance that takes away a depression that you suffer from no matter how happy you ought to be?

Of course, just as there are negative things in every human being's life that they can dwell on if they are depressed due to a chemical imbalance in their minds, there are also things that are genuinely depressing even if there is no chemical imbalance. Alcohol, being a depressant, will also take the edge of these. However, when it wears off, the drinker will not only be left with the depressing event but also the after-effects of the drink, which can only exacerbate the misery. Very simply put, if you have a problem, drinking will not solve it. In fact, it can only make it worse. Things that are genuinely awful but manageable can transform into the genuinely awful and unbearable if you factor in the depressing after-effects of alcohol consumption.

If it is the case that alcohol causes and then relieves this anxiety and depression, then surely virtually everyone would be alcoholic from the off, and there would scarcely be a sober person on the planet? It would also be the case that simply explaining the position would immediately cure any alcoholic or problem drinker (or indeed any other type of drinker). If you are anxious and depressed (for whatever reason) and something relieves this, this won't mean you immediately become addicted to this substance. You may want it to relieve your anxiety and depression if you suffer from it again, but if someone explained that the substance was actually a poison, that if you took it you would lose your job, your house, your friends, your family, your self-respect, and your very life, and in any event it was this substance that was causing the depression, you would most likely stop taking it with little or no problem.

Of course it is not as simple as this. So what are the additional factors that cause something to be 'addictive', i.e. something that you will be forced against your will to take even though it is categorically proven to you that the substance is the cause and not the cure of your problems, and that it will not only kill you but it will rob you of your friends, family, job, home, and self-respect before it does so? To consider this we now need to move from the chemical and physiological to the psychological, in particular our subconscious mind. It is worth remembering as well that while a huge binge will result in a feeling of depression the next day, drinking on a lesser scale will produce a negative impact but on a correspondingly reduced scale. One drink will produce a corresponding feeling of anxiety, but this will be almost imperceptible. Imperceptible to our conscious mind at least, but not to our subconscious.

3.   The Subconscious

The conscious, thinking part of our brain is 17% of the total brain.
The rest is the subconscious. The brain receives approximately
2,000 bits of information per second, and the vast majority of these
are routed to the subconscious. The role of the subconscious is
essentially to process information that you do not have the capacity
to process consciously. It is the subconscious that makes us act
'instinctively'. What does instinctively actually mean other than 'I
know the right thing to do I just don't have a logical reason for it'?

In fact, when you act instinctively there is a logical reason for it,
and the reason is that over the course of your life your subconscious
has been receiving and processing data and it is upon this that an
instinctive decision is made. It is based on trial and error. If you do
something a thousand times with the same result, it will be
programmed into your subconscious. The more you do it, the
deeper it becomes ingrained. In fact, the vast majority of
information that is passed to the subconscious mind is simply
disregarded. It is only when the same or similar data is received
time and again with the same or similar results that it starts to
register on the subconscious, and over time it will become a large
and influential part of our subconscious reasoning. This is how I
can be sitting in the passenger seat of a car and, if the driver is

leaving the braking too late, I find my braking foot tensing. There is no logical reason for it, there is no brake on the passenger side, but for years as a driver my subconscious has absorbed the message that extending my right leg will slow down a vehicle. Another example is whenever I step on an escalator that is not moving. I always lurch even when I know full well in my conscious mind that it is not moving. Although my conscious mind knows the escalator is not moving and that I have to use it as if it were stairs, my subconscious comes up from nowhere and tells me that escalators move and that I need to compensate when I step onto one. My subconscious always wins and I step onto the escalator with exactly the right muscle coordination to meet a moving floor, and as it isn't moving I lurch slightly. The subconscious often wins because it is an extraordinarily strong force and it takes intense concentration to counter it, and when I am walking through a busy commuter station in rush hour I simply do not have the time or inclination to counter my subconscious. We often refer to the subconscious as 'instinct'. It is not, however, instinct (and by that I mean an almost supernatural force causing us to act or react in a certain way); it is based on our personal experience, arising from trial and error over many years.

There are several points to note there. Firstly, the subconscious is extremely powerful and it takes a conscious effort to override it.

Secondly, it is based on trial and error: the more something happens with the same or similar result, the more deeply ingrained this becomes in our subconscious. Finally, it is impossible to know the actual reasons behind the subconscious trigger, nor is it possible to analyse the reasons logically. When I step onto a stationary escalator I don't recall the myriad of times I have stepped onto an escalator that is moving. It is based purely on subconscious memory, and as such each individual occasion making up the subconscious trigger cannot be recalled to the conscious mind.

So what has this to do with alcohol? Simply this: every alcoholic drink any human being has ever drunk has caused a feeling of relaxation followed by a corresponding feeling of anxiety. One drink will cause a very minor and almost unnoticeable feeling of relaxation then anxiety, particularly if we are otherwise occupied at the time (such as if we are socialising or sleeping). Another drink will relieve that very minor feeling of anxiety in addition to any other anxiety we happen to be feeling at the time. This may or may not register on your conscious mind, but it will pass through your subconscious mind. It will pass through your subconscious mind without making an impact the first, second, or third time, but the repetition will eventually be marked by your subconscious mind, which will process the data and form conclusions. And the conclusion will be this: that an alcoholic drink will relieve anxiety and depression. And over the days, weeks, months, and years this message will become more and more reinforced in your subconscious mind until every time you suffer from any stress or anxiety your mind will trigger the instinctive thought that you need an alcoholic drink to relieve the stress and anxiety, and that thought will become stronger and stronger as the message is continually reinforced. Your subconscious mind will recognise that an alcoholic drink will relieve the feelings of anxiety and depression because the drink and the relief will be close together chronologically. You will take a drink and very shortly after this you will experience the relief. However, it will not associate the alcoholic drink with the cause of the anxiety and depression in the first place as it takes far longer for the anxiety and depression to accumulate after the final alcoholic drink has been drunk.

In this way, the subconscious mind misses out this key piece of information: that it was the alcohol that caused the feeling of anxiety in the first place. So although we can understand on a conscious, logical level that it was the alcohol that caused the anxiety in the first place and that alcohol's 'benefit' is in fact to relieve a symptom that it has largely caused, it won't stop us wanting a drink because the subconscious mind will still be triggering a desire for an alcoholic drink every time we feel anxiety or depression, be it caused by alcohol withdrawal or anything else.

The timing between the consuming of a substance and the effect of it is key, not only to understanding alcoholism, but to understanding addiction generally. The quicker the effect of a drug is felt after it is consumed, the quicker the subconscious will link the one with the other and the quicker and more effectively the addiction will take hold. The effect of a drug is felt when it enters the bloodstream, so the quicker this happens after it is consumed, the more addictive it is. In order of speed from quickest to slowest, the methods of consuming a drug are:

1. Injection – which places the drug directly into the bloodstream.

2. Smoking – the smoke diffuses directly into large blood vessels that receive oxygenated blood directly from the lungs and affects the user within less than a second of the first inhalation.

3. Snorting – the drug is absorbed into the bloodstream through the soft tissue in the sinus cavity.

4. Swallowing – this is the slowest method as the drug has to pass through the stomach and into the small intestine before it is absorbed into the bloodstream.

Obviously the almost universal method of consuming alcohol is by swallowing it, with the result that it is one of the drugs that takes longest to become addicted to. In fact, the time lapse between the swallowing of the alcohol to the feeling of the effect of it can itself be greatly varied depending on circumstances, primarily whether our stomachs are full or empty, if we have been exercising, and the strength of the alcoholic drink being consumed (a stronger alcoholic drink will result in a quicker uptake into the bloodstream). This is why so many people prefer drinking before a meal and/or after exercising, and why consumption of spirits (as opposed to wine or beer) is associated with alcoholism. It is also the case that when people start to become dependent on alcohol they often tend to eat less (this is dealt with more fully later in this book) and they become physically debilitated, with the result that alcohol is absorbed into their bloodstreams even faster, and the process of addiction accelerates.

So if we take an alcoholic or a problem drinker and explain to them how alcohol works on a chemical and physiological level only, they may well (and indeed should) conclude that they are better off without drinking and that the only logical thing to do is to stop. However, when they do stop they will suffer anxiety and stress, caused by either alcohol withdrawal in the short term or by the stresses and strains of life generally that every human being suffers from to one degree or another. Whenever they suffer this stress their subconscious will trigger the thought of having an alcoholic drink, and how long these triggers last for will directly depend on how long the individual has been drinking for. The more years a person has been drinking, the more deeply ingrained the subconscious triggers are.

These subconscious triggers explain why some people find they are regularly thinking about alcohol, but ultimately they just trigger the thought of a drink. The thought is no stronger than 'how about having a drink?' It doesn't explain why some people are prepared to give up everything most dear to them (including their very lives) to keep drinking. The reason is that these subconscious triggers in themselves trigger another psychological process known as craving which, when combined with the subconscious triggers, really explains why it is so difficult for some people to stop or control their drinking.

4.   Craving

A craving is an extraordinarily powerful force, and indeed many definitions of alcoholism include the craving for alcohol. A craving is an overwhelming desire for something, and someone who craves alcohol on a regular basis clearly has serious problems. Let's look a bit closer at the psychological process of craving so we can understand it fully before applying it to alcohol.

Let's start by taking an example of something entirely benign. Let's say we crave an apple. Let's look at the psychological factors at play. Right. We want an apple. We can't have one. Either there are none available or (for some reason) we have decided that we would be better off not having one and have resolved not to have one. We can then do one of two things. We can abandon the idea or we can continue to want one. We aren't likely to abandon the idea because we have already decided we want one. It may be that part of us thinks we would be better off without it, but part of our mind must want it or the idea wouldn't have entered into our head in the first place.

So we are now in the position of wanting something we can't have; however, our mind doesn't give up on the idea and we continue to think about having that apple. We dwell on it, we think about it, we fantasise about it, we can't concentrate on anything else, we are miserable because we want something that we cannot have. If we are at work we can't concentrate on our job because we are too busy obsessing about having an apple. If we are at a social function or at home supposedly relaxing for the evening we find we can't enjoy the social function, nor can we relax, because we are too busy obsessing about the apple that we cannot have.

Ultimately, again, we have only two choices: we either give in and have the apple, or we don't. If we give in and have the apple then we have removed the distressing mental conundrum; we can then get on with our work, enjoy the social function, or actually start relaxing at home. That apple has actually been the difference between happiness and misery, the difference between living our lives and having to put them on hold while we are miserable wanting something we can't have. On the other hand, if we don't have the apple then the evening or day is a write-off and for the rest of our lives we will remember how unhappy we were without that apple. So when we next come to crave, the craving will be all the more powerful as we will know from personal experience that we are incapable of enjoying ourselves or functioning without the apple. This process is what I will refer to from here on as 'the spiral of craving'.

Now the craving for an apple is a relatively silly example, but if we were to substitute a chocolate bar or a burger, or any of our favourite foods, it would be a bit more understandable. This would particularly be the case if we were very hungry and were craving our favourite food. The position would be even more pronounced and understandable if there were ample of this food lying around and everyone else was happily tucking into it. In that situation we could not possibly be happy, even if it were a social function at which we were supposed to be enjoying ourselves.

This is essentially the situation faced by the drinker who has stopped drinking. They want something that they cannot have and, moreover, something that they see everyone else enjoying. If they have stopped drinking for some considerable time there is no physical aspect at all, it is entirely mental and is triggered firstly by the subconscious triggers, which set off a desire for something they cannot have, which leads on to the spiral of craving. This can last forever. Every time you want something you can't have you will be miserable, particularly if you see other people enjoying what you can't have. This is why so many people believe that alcoholics have a different genetic make-up from other people. Even after the physical aspect must have ended, the person can find they still can't function fully without a drink. However, it is purely a placebo at this point and is caused by them thinking that they would be happier with a drink, so the spiral of craving starts and they are miserable until they have one.

This is why craving is so powerful. When the thought enters our mind and we start to obsess about it, we won't know a moment's peace until we have it. At this stage, the thing we are obsessing about then starts to take on a life of its own.

Let's consider how this applies to alcohol. Let's say we are feeling anxious or depressed (be it because of alcohol withdrawal or any other reason). Our subconscious will trigger an urge for a drink. If, at this point, we simply take the drink, we have simply relieved a (possibly minor) feeling of anxiety or depression, this will register on our subconscious and this is about the sum total of the effect. However, if we have decided we ought not have a drink for any reason, and we do not take one such that the spiral of craving starts, when we do eventually take the drink we are not only relieving the feeling of anxiety or depression, we are also relieving the mental torture, confusion, and misery of the spiral of craving. This will be registered on our subconscious and conscious mind as well, but crucially from this point on the lesson is not just that a drink will relieve a minor feeling of anxiety, but that having an alcoholic drink is the most important thing on God's earth, and without it we simply cannot function or ever be happy ever again.

This is actually a part of the process of becoming addicted to alcohol. When we try to stop drinking, the spiral of craving starts and the drink relieves this, along with any minor feelings of anxiety. Many people believe that the drinker who tries to stop and cannot is already fully addicted to alcohol; the attempt and subsequent failure to stop is simply evidence of this. In fact, the process of attempting to stop actually takes the already existing addiction to a new level. It is when we try to stop that the spiral of craving starts, and from then on the lesson being absorbed by the subconscious is not that alcohol provides a neat remedy to anxiety and depression, but that if we want a drink and cannot have one we literally cannot function as a human being.

There are two points to note at this stage. Firstly, that the spiral of craving is the backbone of any addiction. The subconscious triggers themselves are brief; they are literally just knee-jerk reactions to a given situation. They trigger the thought of an alcoholic drink, no more than that. However, these subconscious triggers often start us thinking very consciously about having a drink, and our thought process is usually about how nice it would be to have a drink, of taking that ice-cold beer out of the fridge, or pouring that glass of wine or that measure of our favourite spirit. Soon we find ourselves fantasising about having a drink, and the craving is in full sway. It is the craving that creates the mental agony we encounter when trying to give anything up. The bad news is that it is an extremely powerful force and that this is why addicts find it so hard to give up the objects of their addiction. However, the very good news is that craving takes place entirely in the conscious mind, and therefore we face a conscious decision whether to crave or not. How to overcome the spiral of craving is dealt with in more detail later in this book.

The other, very important point to note is that when alcohol starts to become a problem and the drinker tries to stop and fails, the failure is due to their wanting to avoid the spiral of craving. They are not, at this stage, drinking for the supposed benefits of drinking, but rather they are drinking to avoid the misery of the craving. It is entirely negative. Without alcohol they cannot function or be happy because of the craving; with alcohol they avoid the craving, but this means they are no better off than had they never had a drink. In fact, they are far worse off because, as we all know, with alcohol they face all the problems associated with drinking: the hangovers, the relationship problems, the loss of health, self-respect, etc. So in fact they are utterly miserable without the drink thanks to the craving, and only slightly less miserable with it. It is a lose/lose situation for them.

However, even when we understand and appreciate the effects of the physical withdrawal, the subconscious triggers, and the spiral of craving, we still don't have a full explanation. If this was all there was to it then alcohol wouldn't be a problem, even for the chronic alcoholic. They would have a drink and, when it started to wear off, they would simply need to top it up with another. They would never be entirely sober, but equally they would have no reason to become utterly intoxicated. So let's now move on to the next piece of the jigsaw puzzle: the relaxing effects of alcohol.

5.   The Relaxing Effects of Alcohol

If you ask anyone (be they a drinker or a teetotaller) why a person takes a drink, the most common answer is that a person drinks for the relaxing, comforting effect. Alcohol is a depressant and an anaesthetic; it anaesthetises certain feelings (such as tiredness, stress, pain, and discomfort) and the effect of this is that we tend to feel more mentally relaxed after a drink. Of course, the depressant/anaesthetising effects don't just work on our mind, causing us to feel relaxed; they also affect the rest of our body, leaving us slightly uncoordinated and slow. This is the effect of one or two drinks; if we increase our intake then we increase the effects on both sides, and this can lead to full-blown intoxication.

It has always been assumed that the relaxing mental effect and the physical impairment or intoxication go hand in hand, that they are part and parcel of the same process. However, this is not the case. The physical intoxication and the mental relaxation run their course at different speeds.

To give an example of this, where many people encounter problems with drink driving laws is that after a night of heavy drinking they can be over the limit when driving the following morning. It takes the average human one hour to process one unit of alcohol (a unit being approximately half a pint of beer or a single measure of spirits), so you can quite easily see how you could be over the limit for driving the following day, particularly if you have drunk a lot the night before and if you live in a country with a zero tolerance rule (i.e. where you are allowed no alcohol in your system at all while driving).

But, and this is a really key point, most people caught drink driving the following day do not feel drunk. They genuinely think that they are sober. In fact, it is only those who have not been drinking for very long, or those who usually drink modest amounts and then have a big binge, who still feel actually drunk the morning after. This is because their bodies have not yet learnt to efficiently counter the amount of alcohol that has been imbibed. Most people who still have alcohol in their system the morning after drinking will be physically intoxicated but will not have any corresponding feeling of alcohol-induced mental relaxation.

To go into further detail, most people, when they wake up the following morning still under the influence of the previous night's drinking, won't feel like they do when they have just had a drink one evening. If you wake up after a night's drinking with two beers' worth of alcohol in your bloodstream, you will not feel like you would if you had two pints of beer after work one day. In the latter situation you will feel the relaxing effects of the drink. You may not be drunk but you will know you've had a drink. However, when you have that amount in your system from the night before (or even a considerably larger amount), you will feel stone cold sober in that there is no feeling of relaxation. However, although you may feel mentally sober, you are not physically sober. Your reactions are as slowed as they would be if you had the drinks at the end of the day. So you can feel mentally sober but be physically intoxicated.

This is a very obvious example of how physical intoxication and a feeling of mental relaxation run their course at different speeds, with the intoxicating effect outlasting the relaxing effect. It is obvious because it is exaggerated by several hours' abstention from alcohol in the form of a night's sleep. However, the same effect occurs with every drink we consume and the process occurs in the same way during the course of a night's drinking, only on a less obvious scale.

So, if we are drinking for the relaxing mental effect, we have to keep the drinks coming faster than the wearing off of the physical intoxication. To put it another way, if we decide that we like the relaxing effect two drinks have on us, then when this relaxing effect wears off we will need to take two further drinks to replenish the effect. However, the physical intoxication won't have worn off, so we'll be two drinks mentally relaxed but four drinks physically intoxicated. Then when the relaxing mental effect of those two drinks wears off, and we take two more, we'll be two drinks mentally relaxed but now six drinks physically intoxicated. It may be that by this time your body will have processed the physical intoxication effect of a single drink, but even so you will still be two drinks relaxed but five drinks intoxicated.

This is how we can wake up the morning after a heavy night and still be physically intoxicated even though the relaxing effects of the drink are long gone. This is also why virtually every drinker that has ever lived has had at least one occasion where they have inadvertently consumed too much alcohol. In fact, not only has virtually every single drinker consumed too much alcohol on occasion, but the vast majority have done so on several occasions and continue to do so throughout their drinking lives. Drinkers have to exercise caution about drinking too much. Do they have the same problems with coffee, tea, water, or soft drinks? If a husband or wife is going out one evening for a drink it is commonplace for their partner to issue a warning about drinking too much, but if the person was going out for a coffee do they ever get told 'Please make sure you don't have too many, you know you get very shaky and can't sleep when you have too much caffeine'?

Now is a good time to stop and summarise where we are. Essentially, alcohol provides us with a feeling of relaxation. However, the brain and nervous system reacts to this by releasing stimulants and becoming more sensitive, with the result that when the alcohol wears off we are more anxious and unrelaxed than we were before we took the drink. So we are inclined to take another drink, and the relaxing effect of every drink we take registers on the subconscious, but the corresponding feeling of anxiety does not register on the subconscious as being the result of the alcohol as it is too far apart in time for the subconscious to link the one with the other. So over time the subconscious mind comes to believe that alcohol will relieve anxiety, so that whenever we suffer anxiety or stress in our lives we encounter a subconscious trigger to take a drink. This in turn can set off the spiral of craving, which means we simply cannot function or enjoy ourselves without a drink. All the while and throughout this entire process, as the body and brain become increasingly proficient at countering the alcohol, the mental relaxation is increasingly outstripped by the physical intoxication, meaning we are increasingly inclined to lose control when we are drinking and end up totally intoxicated.

However, there are some further key aspects we will need to consider so we can build up a full understanding of alcohol. One of the most important and one of the least well known of these is the effect alcohol has on sleep.

6.   Alcohol and Sleep

Although it is largely accepted in academic and medical circles that alcohol has an adverse effect on sleep, this seems to be largely unknown among the general public. Sleep deprivation is an awful thing. There has been a recent article in the press stating that Scientists from Oxford, Cambridge, Harvard, Manchester, and Surrey universities warn that cutting sleep leads to 'serious health problems', that cancer, heart disease, type-2 diabetes, infections, and obesity have all been linked to reduced sleep, and that lack of sleep will affect alertness, mood, and physical strength. I am not sure this is news as such; it is just sound common sense. When we sleep our body repairs itself. If we are not getting enough or the right quality of sleep, our body won't be properly repairing itself and we will quickly decline, both physically and mentally. Bearing in mind how important sleep is, it is essential that we give full consideration to the effect alcohol has on our sleep.

One of the main reasons that alcohol's negative effect on sleep is not widely acknowledged is that everyone knows a drink or two can make you feel sleepy. It is therefore generally accepted that alcohol aids sleep. However, this is a fallacy. Normally (i.e. without the introduction of alcohol into the system), a person goes through two alternating states of sleep. These states are called slow wave sleep

(SWS) and rapid eye movement (REM) sleep. Slow wave sleep is the deep, restful sleep. REM sleep, however, is less restful and is usually associated with dreaming.

Although its function is unknown, REM appears to be as essential to health as SWS sleep. In tests with rats, deprivation of REM sleep has led to death within a few weeks. Equally, SWS sleep is essential as this is when the body actually restores itself. There is a lot we, as human beings, do not know about sleep; however, what is certainly the case is that the human body needs certain cycles of sleep and those that occur naturally are those that are most beneficial for us. Interfere with these and we cause ourselves serious problems.

If we allow these cycles of sleep to occur naturally, the result will usually be that we wake up feeling refreshed and ready for the day. In a natural cycle of sleep you will have six or seven cycles of REM sleep. However, when you drink you will typically only have two. The reason for this is that when we drink we go into a very deep sleep for the first five hours or so. You would be forgiven for thinking that this is a good thing, as we would usually associate a deep sleep with an invigorating and refreshing sleep, but this is not the case. The initial five hours or so of drinking sleep do not have enough REM sleep. The other problem is that after the initial five hours or so the deep sleep ends and the rest of our sleep is very fragmented. This five-hour period is very important as this is when the alcohol withdrawal starts to peak. This point is dealt with in more detail elsewhere in this book.

However, sticking with sleep for the time being, this is why many drinkers will find that they will usually wake up around five hours after they have taken their last drink, after which they will sleep fitfully if at all and will not go into deep sleep again. The practical upshot of this is that when waking up after drinking we do not feel refreshed and well rested even if we are not actually 'hung over' per se. This is why you will so often hear people saying, 'I am not hung over, just a bit tired'. If the definition of a hangover is the ill effects of the previous night's drinking, then that tiredness is most certainly a part of the hangover. You need to get this straight in your mind: alcohol ruins sleep. If you are tired the next day, this is as a direct result of the previous night's drinking. Even one drink will interrupt the natural sleeping pattern, and there is no safe amount to drink which will allow you to escape the ill effects of drinking as it impacts sleep.

I know that many drinkers claim to sleep better, or at least to have no worse sleep when drinking, but the simple fact is that if they drink they will not be obtaining the good quality sleep they need. Even if you go spark out for eight or ten hours, your body will not be going through the sleep cycles it needs, it will not be getting enough REM sleep, and it will not be able to go into deep sleep after about five hours. You may wake up feeling what you think is fine, but the inescapable fact is that you would feel that much better had you not drunk the night before. You also need to bear in mind that the ill effects of sleep deprivation are accumulative. Most people will be able to go a night or two without having a proper sleep with minimal noticeable ill effects, particularly if they are young. Indeed, if you are sleeping well then the odd night here and there will have virtually no negative impact at all. However, over consecutive nights the problems will increase: the less sleep you get the worse the symptoms become.

When we are suffering from sleep deprivation we are not only in a state of constant tiredness, but our mental and physical capacity also decreases. This has an entirely detrimental effect on our lives and our physical and mental well-being. Sleep deprivation also tends to make us more short tempered, more inclined to let things get on top of us, more prone to overeat, and less inclined to exercise. It also makes us more prone to do two other things that are key when looking to build up a complete understanding of alcohol.

The first of the things that tiredness makes us more prone to do is to take a drink. After all, alcohol is a depressant and an anaesthetic, so it will alleviate feelings of tiredness and the ever-increasing feeling of exhaustion. We feel tired, we have a drink, then suddenly we don't feel so tired anymore. In fact the person who was, moments ago, vowing to go to bed at the first opportunity, suddenly thinks it seems like a very good idea to sit up a bit longer and have another drink. Again this may not seem like a bad thing, but we have to remember that the feeling of suddenly having more energy is false. The body is still tired, it still needs rest and proper sleep, but because the signals telling us this have been depressed we carry on. At some point we go to bed, we sleep, the alcohol wears off, our sleep is disrupted yet again, and we wake up feeling worse than ever. We have not had the rest we need, our bodies are also then coping with the poisoning effect of the alcohol, and the position the next day is worsened considerably.

The other thing that tiredness makes us more prone to do that is of particular relevance to alcohol is to take (more) stimulants during the day to counteract the feeling of exhaustion. Those of us who drink caffeinated drinks will find we tend to consume more of them when we are tired, and those who smoke will find they smoke more. The increased stimulants we imbibe will make us feel even more uptight and irritable. Of course, there will also be naturally occurring stimulants and stress hormones in our system after drinking. Adrenaline and other chemicals that the brain releases into our system when we feel stressed are stimulants. The combination of this will mean we are left feeling much more uptight and irritable, two classic unpleasant feelings that are quite easily relieved by drinking.

The other problem with modern living is that the naturally occurring stimulants developed in the days when stress was usually a physical threat and these chemicals would give us the ability to conjure a stronger physical reaction, either to fight or run away. That fight or flight, being a physical thing, would work some of these chemicals out of our system.

However, these days, for most people in Western society, the things that cause stress on a day-to-day basis do not warrant a physical reaction. We feel stressed at work because we have too much on, we receive the adrenaline rush but we don't react to having a last-minute report to write by running out of the office or attacking our boss (tempting as either of those options often are). We sit and get on with it, and although we are mentally stressed we are physically inactive, so by the end of the day we have an excess of unused adrenaline in our bodies leaving us feeling uncomfortable, irritable, and tense. We either put up with this feeling and let it slowly dissipate, take a little exercise to work it out of our system, or we have a drink. The last of these options is often the easiest option and the one so many of us turn to. A drink not only relieves the tense feeling, but also the feeling of exhaustion.

This may not seem like a bad thing to many people; however, we need to bear in mind that this tiredness and tenseness have been greatly exacerbated or even out-and-out caused by alcohol in the first place.

It is also worth keeping in mind that a disrupted sleep pattern takes time to repair. Think of sleep as a habit that takes a few nights to form. People will often claim to sleep badly whether they drink or not. This usually comes from people who drink regularly (i.e. most days) and have the odd day off here or there and still sleep badly. This is because for people who drink regularly, their sleep pattern is regularly disrupted. If they stop on day one they may well have a very poor night's sleep that night, indeed it is likely to be even worse than had they been drinking. Nights two, three, and even four will be increasingly better but often not perfect, but usually by day five the body has fully adjusted and something akin to normal sleep is resumed. However, even then it can take some time before the body starts to catch up on the missed, good quality sleep. If you have not had a good night's sleep for a month, you are not going to catch up in one night. It will take quite a few nights of proper sleep before you get even close to being back on par. Very few (if any) regular drinkers take drinking breaks for long enough to firstly remedy the broken sleeping pattern and secondly to catch up on the lost sleep, which means that they never properly remedy the ill effects. In fact, what they do is to continually exacerbate the problem by continuing to drink.

There is one final point worth mentioning for anyone who uses alcohol each night to get to sleep, or to combat insomnia. If you don't drink, when you are getting ready to sleep clusters of sleep-promoting neurons in many parts of the brain become more active and certain chemicals are released that dampen the activity of cells that signal arousal. What this actually means is when you are getting towards sleep, your brain starts to wind down, and you start to feel naturally sleepy. However, when you drink every night to induce sleep, your brain simply doesn't trigger this naturally occurring 'winding down' process. After all, why would it? It is used to relying on the depressing effects of the alcohol to get you off to sleep. It has adjusted to the daily amount of alcohol. However, just as it has adjusted to having it, it will also adjust to not having it, but it will take a few days. Again, you will be looking at three to five days for the readjustment.

7.   Dehydration

Some theories of alcohol addiction state that it is alcohol's dehydrating effect that causes us to want to keep drinking when we start (the argument being that you have a drink, it makes you thirsty, so you drink another). Let's now examine this, and consider the effects of dehydration generally.

The average human body is around 70% water. The actual water content is controlled by the brain, which keeps a certain percentage as a reserve in case it is suddenly required, usually for sweating. Sweating is one of the ways in which our bodies maintain the correct temperature (sweating places moisture on the skin which removes heat from the skin as it evaporates); however, even when we are not actively sweating, we still use water – for example in respiration.

The actual amount of the reserve we need is not a constant. In this, as with everything else, the body reacts to the world around it and the particular situation it is in. If the ambient temperature drops then in a fairly short space of time the brain will react to this. The brain concludes that due to the drop in temperature, sweating is going to be less likely or less extreme so the excess water that the brain requires as a backup decreases. The body then rids itself of the unrequired excess through urination, which is why we often find we need to urinate when the temperature drops, even if we haven't drunk any liquid for some time.

It is also the case that when this water reserve drops below a certain level, thirst is triggered. In this way, the body/brain sends the message that more water is needed, we drink, and the reserve levels of water are topped up. The entire process works by way of the body gauging the level of reserve water required compared to what it currently holds.

The easiest way of picturing this is to think of the fuel gauge on a car. It shows how much fuel is in the tank, and if the fuel drops below a certain level, usually a red light comes on as an additional warning. In the same way, your body has a gauge that determines the level of reserve water, and when this level drops below a certain level the thirst mechanism is triggered.

What alcohol does is to mess around with the operation of that gauge; specifically, it recalibrates it in such a way that your body thinks it has more water than it actually has. To go back to the car analogy, it is like recalibrating the fuel gauge so that the gauge shows full when the fuel tank is in fact half empty. In fact, the analogy with the car isn't ideal because a fuel gauge can only swing

53

from empty to full, it cannot jettison additional fuel if the gauge showed that the tank had somehow been overfilled. However, this is exactly what happens with the human body. The human body will jettison the reserve if it assesses that it has an unwanted excess of reserve water. Of course, when the effect of the alcohol wears off, the gauge is reset back to the correct level. The body then realises that it does not have enough reserve water and it looks to replenish this supply. It does this by triggering the thirst mechanism, we drink some liquid, and the supply is topped up to the correct level. The important point to note is that the internal gauge will not return to normal until the effect of the alcohol has worn off.

Let's now look at a practical example to highlight this by looking at a hypothetical person with a 100% correct water reserve, i.e. at that particular point in time they are perfectly hydrated in that they have all the water they need but no more (so they do not need to urinate). They then start drinking alcohol. Now, apart from the fact that alcohol is consumed as a liquid which will need to be urinated out, the alcohol also recalibrates their internal water gauge with the effect that a percentage of the reserve water is also expelled. This is why after a few drinks we start needing the toilet increasingly regularly and we do not just urinate out the exact amount of liquid that we consumed, but much more as our body also rids itself of (what it thinks is) an unwanted excess of reserve water. The next morning, or during the course of the next day (if we are not consuming more alcohol), the effect slowly wears off and the body gauges that it does not have enough reserve water and we start to feel thirsty. If we take a (non-alcoholic) drink, we replenish the water and start to return to normal.

As I have mentioned previously, the important point to note is that the gauge is not recalibrated back to the correct position until the alcohol wears off. The important conclusion to note from this is that we will not feel thirsty as a result of the dehydration until the thing that has caused the recalibration of our internal water gauge has worn off. After all, why would our body be triggering the thirst mechanism when it is under the impression that we have the correct amount of water anyway? In this way we do not feel thirsty when we are actually drinking alcohol because the thirst mechanism is not triggered because, in turn, our body does not realise that it does not have enough water in it. You do not feel thirsty when you are dehydrated due to alcohol consumption until the effect of the alcohol has worn off.

The further conclusion of this is that it is absolutely pointless trying to rehydrate yourself during a drinking session or immediately after it (such as on the way home). A friend of mine used to drink a couple of bottles of water on the way home after drinking in the hope that it would rehydrate him and ward off a hangover. In fact, doing this will have done absolutely nothing at all other than disturb his already severely hampered sleep still further by causing him to need the toilet even more during the night. His body would not have kept hold of any of the water he drank, even though it was dehydrated at that point, because it was acting under the erroneous impression that it already had an adequate water content. It is only when the effect of the alcohol has worn off and the thirst mechanism is actually triggered that the water will be retained by the body and actually put to use, as it is at this point that the internal water gauge has returned to its correct position. You will always know when the gauge is returning to normal because you will begin to feel genuinely thirsty again.

This is why exercising after drinking, or exercising with a hangover, is so dangerous. Not only is it the case that the body simply doesn't have the reserve of liquid to deal with strenuous exercise (which causes both sweating and increased respiration), but the internal water gauge is still malfunctioning so the body doesn't even realise there is a problem (i.e. hydration levels have dropped to critical levels) until it is too late. When the body recognises that the water level is low it will send us messages telling us we will feel thirsty, hot, and exhausted, and we will be forced to stop what we are doing. However, if the body is not aware that the level is too low, the messages telling us to stop, to cool down, to drink water, will not be triggered.

8.   Taste

Many people believe they like the taste of alcohol. They may like the taste of alcoholic drinks, but they do not like the taste of alcohol. This may seem to be a contradiction in terms but not if we consider alcohol in its purest form and also the chemical make-up of alcoholic drinks.

Alcohol in its pure form is a highly poisonous chemical. It is a toxin that kills living things, from human beings to single cells and microorganisms, which is why it is used to preserve food and to sterilise. It sterilises by killing the germs it comes into contact with. It doesn't just kill germs, it kills all living cells. In fact, for humans the toxicity is increased because in order for it to be cleared from the body it has to be metabolised to acetaldehyde, an even more toxic substance. Any food or drink contaminated with the amount of acetaldehyde that a unit of alcohol produces would be banned as having an unacceptable health risk.

The human body is designed to be repulsed by poison. It is a mechanism which keeps us alive. There are some poisons which our bodies don't recognise as such and the result is that we are not repulsed by them. However, alcohol is most certainly not one of these. It is a poison, and our body reacts to it as a poison. If you sniff neat alcohol it will make your eyes water and your nose run, and your immediate reaction will be to shy away from it. If you sip it you will retch; if you do manage to swallow any you will start vomiting. All these reactions are your body's way of stopping you from imbibing it, and getting it out of your body if you do manage somehow to consume some. Your body is designed to prevent you from harming yourself. It is much the same reaction that would cause you to snatch your hand away from something that you inadvertently touched that was burning hot. Pain does not feel nice. People avoid pain. Pain is caused by damage to our bodies. In this way, the body works to prevent us from injuring ourselves.

So how can I conclude that it is impossible to like that taste of alcohol, but in the same sentence say that it is possible to like the taste of alcoholic drinks? The reason for this is that alcoholic drinks are not pure alcohol; in fact, the alcoholic content of any alcoholic drink is only a small percentage. They also contain some other very strong flavours that largely mask the taste of the alcohol.

So if you drink a beer that is 4% vol. only a twenty-fifth of it is alcohol. A glass of wine of 12% is only three parts out of twenty-five alcohol, and a neat spirit of 40% is only two-fifths alcohol. If it is mixed with ice and/or a mixer (as spirits usually are), this percentage in the drink will correspondingly drop. The higher the alcohol content, the more unpalatable the drink.

The point to bear in mind is that alcohol in its pure form is repulsive and highly poisonous to living creatures, no human being is capable of ingesting it without vomiting, and if it can be kept down it is usually fatal. Even spirits (which are considered strong drinks such that most people will only imbibe them with ice or a mixer) are not even half alcohol, and beers and wines have a very small percentage of alcohol in them. The vast majority of alcoholic drinks are made up of non-alcoholic substances, most of which are incredibly strong-tasting in their own right. So when you drink a beer, the taste actually comes from the hops, barley, sugar, etc. with only a tiny amount of that taste coming from the alcohol. With wine it is the grape juice with which it is made. With whiskey it is the barley, rye, and wheat with which it is made and the barrels it is stored in before it is bottled and sold. Increase the alcohol and all you do is make the drink more unpalatable. This is why most people who drink spirits add a mixer. All they are doing is watering down still further the taste of the alcohol in the drink.

Essentially, any alcoholic drink is something that tastes pleasant (for example grape juice) with a very small amount of vile-tasting poison in it such that the drink as a whole is rendered palatable due to the good-tasting part of it far outweighing the vile-tasting poison. In the same way, if you put a small amount of dog urine in a glass of orange juice it would be palatable, providing the amount of urine was small enough that the pleasant taste of the orange masked it adequately!

This is also why most alcoholic drinks are served cold. To delve into the chemistry a bit more, everything (alcoholic drinks included) is made up of molecules. The warmer something is, the more the molecules it is made up of vibrate. The more they vibrate and move, the more they collide. A chemical reaction is simply when the molecules of two substances collide. If the molecules that make up the two substances are warmer, they will be moving faster and will collide all the more, which will result in the chemical reaction speeding up and the results being all the more noticeable.

Taste is simply a chemical reaction between receptors in the mouth and whatever substance we are consuming. If the substance we are eating or drinking is very cold we will be able to actually taste it less than if it were warm or hot, as the molecules which it is made up of will collide less with the receptors in our mouths. If we chill something before drinking it, all we are doing is negating the actual taste of it. If you find a drink unpalatable when it is warm, then beware: there is probably something in it that your body is averse to the taste of, most likely because it is a poison. Of course, there are several alcoholic drinks that are drunk warm, such as red wine, mulled wine, hot toddies, etc., but these tend to have even stronger flavours than other alcoholic drinks.

Finally, it is also worth bearing in mind that if we continually imbibe something unpalatable, our sense of smell and taste become immune to it. For example, no one can enjoy very spicy food without first getting used to it. All 'getting used to it' really means is that the sense of smell and taste becomes abraded such that higher amounts can be tolerated. The more the sensitivity in respect of certain substances is reduced, the more of that substance we can imbibe. So if you drink red wine now but when you started drinking you would drink cold white wine, or if you can drink neat whiskey but would never have been able to do so when you started drinking, all that has happened is that you are less able to detect the poison within the drink that your body is naturally repulsed by.

9.   **Alcohol and Fitness**

Have you ever wondered what the physical difference is between people who are fit and people who are unfit? The obvious answer is that fitter people have bigger muscles, but is this really the case? After all, some athletes, for example long distance runners, don't have huge, bulging muscles, but are incredibly fit nonetheless. So what is the physical state of fitness? Interestingly, much of it is to do with the blood.

Essentially our blood contains red blood cells, and it is these cells that carry oxygen and other nutrients to our muscles and organs. People who are physically fit have a greater concentration of red blood cells in their blood, and these tend to be younger, which means they are better at carrying oxygen. This is one of the main characteristic of 'fitness'.

Our muscles require oxygen to keep moving. The heart pumps the blood round our bodies and the red blood cells in the blood deliver the oxygen. When we exercise, our muscles require more oxygen, so the heart speeds up to keep up with the increased demand. The heart, however, can only go so fast, and when it reaches its maximum capacity we are literally incapable of increasing or maintaining that level of exercise. If you regularly increase your heart rate through exercise, the red blood cells become more concentrated. They also have a shorter life span, so your red blood cells are younger and more efficient at carrying the oxygen. Thus, each pump of the heart delivers more oxygen. This has two results. Firstly, we can exercise at higher and higher levels. Secondly, our resting heart rate becomes lower and lower. This is because each pump of the heart delivers more oxygen, so it has to beat less regularly. Of course, the converse is also true. If we are regularly pushing our heart rate up without any related physical activity then each pump of the heart is delivering too much oxygen, so the red blood cells will space out and their life span will increase and consequently they will carry less oxygen. It is the reverse of getting fit; it is a way of actively becoming unfit.

So how do you get your heart rate up without exercising? Stress, of course, will do this (adrenaline increases heart rate), but another very common way of doing this is to take drugs that increase our heart rate. Alcohol can slow the heart rate down while we are drinking it, but it sends it through the roof when the alcohol wears off. This is yet more proof of the physiological effect of drinking; that the stimulants released by the brain to counter the depressive effects of the alcohol remain after the alcohol has been processed. Generally speaking, depressants will slow the heart rate down, while stimulants will increase it. So during the drinking session the heart rate may increase a bit but won't be greatly accelerated, but when you wake up at four in the morning your heart will be going at such a rate that it will feel like it is about to burst out of your chest, and that increased heart rate will follow you around for the following 24–48 hours until the stimulants are finally dispersed. This is a physical manifestation of the stimulants remaining after the alcohol has largely dissipated.

In this way drinking regularly actually erodes our fitness, and this is to say nothing of the general lethargy drinking causes which is, in itself, a bar to exercise. And of course if you are actually hung-over you are not going to manage that training session, and if you do force yourself to do it, it is going to be that much more difficult and that much less intense. And if one of the goals of your fitness routine is weight loss then you also need to then factor in the very clear link between drinking and obesity, which I deal with in more detail later on.

People often view drinking and its effect on health as a hit or miss affair. If your liver doesn't conk out, or if you don't have a crushing heart attack, or a killer stroke, you get away with it scot-free. But this isn't the case. Every drink you consume erodes your fitness. A lack of fitness doesn't just impact your life span; it also impacts your quality of life. Physical well-being is very closely related to mental resilience. It is also worth bearing in mind that this is just one aspect of the health effects of drinking; it doesn't even factor in the effects of the sleep deprivation, the constant poisoning, the increased blood pressure, and the effect of the alcohol related nutritional deficiencies, which we will come on to shortly.

10.   Alcohol's Effect on Emotions

This chapter and the next centre around alcohol's effect on the limbic system. The limbic system is a set of six inner structures in the human brain and is believed to be the emotional centre of the brain. It is believed that the function of the limbic system is to control our emotions and behaviour and is also believed to be responsible for forming long-term memories. Being a chemical depressant, alcohol inhibits the working of the limbic system with the effect that drinking affects both our long-term memory and our emotional state. In this chapter we will consider the impact this has on our emotional state.

There is a phrase in the UK: being 'tired and emotional'. It is a euphemism for being drunk. It originated in the Houses of Parliament, where it was unacceptable to accuse an MP of being drunk. It was obviously equally unacceptable for MPs to remain sober for any length of time, so a euphemism was coined to explain when an MP was drunk without describing them as such. Hence this phrase coming into general use.

In fact, it is a fairly good euphemism for being drunk. Drinking not only causes us to be tired, it also causes us to be overly emotional.

There is a high correlation between alcohol and anger, violence and violent crime. There are also the fairly stereotypical images of the teary drunk crying into their drink and the regretful drunk calling their ex at three in the morning.

A lot of people assume (quite erroneously) that the reason people tend to become emotional when they drink is because alcohol removes our inhibitions so that our 'true' selves come out when we are drunk, and we think and say things that we really feel and believe but that we wouldn't have the courage, or would be too inhibited to say or feel, when we are sober. So the husband who loses his temper with his wife after he has been drinking and either says something hurtful to her or physically attacks her, does so because that is what he really wants to do or say to her, but without alcohol inside him he is too inhibited to act on these feelings. Equally, the call made to the ex at three in the morning is purely because the drunken party really, deep down, wants that person back but is too inhibited, shy, or afraid to act on that feeling without alcohol.

Although this makes sense on one level, the truth is, in fact, completely the other way round. All regular drinkers have lost their temper over something, or had an argument or even a fight when they were drunk, and been completely unable to explain or justify it when they remembered it the following day. And by this I don't mean that they don't understand why they reacted so aggressively, but that they have absolutely no idea why the triggering event affected them at all.

The fact of the matter is that alcohol acts to inhibit certain reactors in the brain that themselves act to put a stop on certain emotions when they take hold. For example, say we are sober and we accidentally break something. We are annoyed, but we clear it up and move on. In this situation anger is triggered in the brain but is then very quickly inhibited as the occurrence that triggered our anger was a minor thing and there was nothing to be gained by completely losing our temper. However, when the same thing happens when we have been drinking, the loss of temper simply runs unchecked because the inhibitor which ought to check the loss of temper has been depressed by our alcohol intake. As any drinker (be they alcoholic, problem, heavy, or otherwise) worth their salt will know, it needn't be anything as obvious as breaking something; it could be a throw-away comment, a look, a completely benign joke. Anything that has the capacity to cause us even minor irritation can lead to a complete and disproportionate loss of temper.

Of course, it is not just loss of temper or anger that is triggered, as any emotion is equally likely to run away with us for the same reason. Drunks can become more teary, more sentimental, more introspective, or more self-pitying. Any emotion can run unchecked when we are drinking. If (like me) you are someone who is generally not very tolerant and is prone to anger anyway, then of course you are more likely to encounter a minor annoyance when you have been drinking that will turn into a full-on fit of rage. Conversely, if you are someone who is prone to sentimentality or tears generally, or if you are feeling unhappy when you start drinking on a particular occasion, then you are more likely to spiral out of control in this way. Anger tends to be a common emotion among drinkers as the lack of good quality sleep, which leaves them feeling tired and drained, is in itself conducive to anger. Aren't we all more inclined to lose our temper when we are tired? Also, the anxious feeling left behind when the effect of an alcoholic drink wears off is also conducive to anger and losing your temper. All in all, it's a fairly explosive cocktail (pun intended).

The simple fact of the matter is that people do not become angry, introspective, unhappy, regretful, or anything else when they drink because the alcohol has brought out the true side of them, but because the alcohol has prevented their brain from acting as it ought to. It changes them into something that they aren't by stopping their brain from working in the way it normally would. Essentially, it causes people to be overly emotional because it causes them to be unable to check their emotions.

In some ways this can be one of the most dreadful and damaging parts of alcohol consumption. It can destroy love, not only for the partner of the drinker but also for the drinker themselves. Any couple will face ups and downs during their relationship, and sometimes they will find their partner infuriating, but overall there is a feeling of love and tolerance. We overlook our partner's shortfalls because we love them and know them to be a good person, and they do the same for us. If they do something we find irritating, we will overlook it because we know it was done accidentally or with the best intentions.

However, if we have been drinking we won't be able to overlook it, or gloss over it, or ignore it. The chances are that we will end up having an argument over it, and it will be an argument we would not have had if we had not been drinking. We will end up being annoyed with our partner and they will end up being annoyed and upset with us. In fact, they are likely to be even more annoyed and upset because they will be able to see quite clearly that it is something we would not have got annoyed over had we not been drinking. We won't be able to see that ourselves, we will just know that they have annoyed us. There will be anger and ill-feeling that would not have existed had we not been drinking. I remember reading a book once where the author compared a marriage to a tower where every argument and bad word is a blow to that tower. Some towers are stronger than others, but all towers can take only a finite amount of battering before they are structurally weakened and come crashing down.

Alcohol can cause relationships to fail that ought otherwise to flourish and grow strong, causing both the drinker and their partner to miss out on what would otherwise be a loving, supportive and successful relationship. This isn't just true of relationships between the drinker and their partners, but also between them and their children, their friends and their relatives. It is like the old films where the baddie hates the hero so much that it is not enough to just kill him; first he has to destroy his reputation and make everyone hate and fear him.

This aspect of drinking is also one of the many anomalies of alcohol consumption. Often a drinking session will be triggered by an unpleasant or negative emotion such as anger, upset, distress, sadness, etc. Being an anaesthetic, alcohol will take the edge off this triggering emotion in the short term, so that the immediate effect of a drink is to make us feel better as we will feel less angry, upset, or whatever. But of course as the reactors in the brain that put a brake on our emotions are themselves anaesthetised, the original emotion that kicked off the drinking in the first place starts to run unchecked. The result of this is that we end up more angry, upset or distressed (or whatever the triggering emotion was) even when we are in the middle of the drinking session, to say nothing of the following morning when we not only have the original problem but also the additional hangover, alcohol withdrawal, and disturbed sleep to contend with. Each drink does provide us with an actual short-term boost, but this is outweighed entirely by the effect on the limbic system, with the effect that very soon we are far angrier than we were to begin with, even while we are actually 'enjoying' the 'relief' provided by the drink.

This actually makes perfect sense if you think about it. If you think that alcohol relieves anger, misery, frustration, etc., then alcoholics (who drink the most) would surely be the happiest people on the planet. Drunks would be the most calm and happy people, and those least likely to get into a fight. This is clearly not the case. There is a very big difference between people drinking to relieve negative emotions (which they clearly do) and alcohol actually relieving negative emotions (which it clearly does not; in fact, it does completely the opposite by greatly exaggerating them).

73

It is very important to also bear in mind that the subconscious will only recognise the effect of alcohol relieving our anger, stress, upset etc, and will not recognise the overall increase in these emotions as this accumulates far more slowly. This is how we can end up in this very strange situation where we all know that alcohol makes people far more emotionally unstable, yet we still all 'instinctively' reach for a drink to relieve our anger, stress, upset, etc.

The fact is that whoever you are as a drinker, it is not the real you. It is a poor quality you. It is a tired, irritable and overly emotional you. Essentially, it is not a very pleasant you. Even if the emotion that runs unchecked is one that we would usually consider to be a positive one, like humour, it is still irritating for other people. A drinker who finds something hilarious that no one else finds the least bit amusing is just as irritating as the miserable drinker, or one who loses their temper over everything. It is also well worth bearing in mind that it is very rarely a positive emotion that runs unchecked, particularly for long-term heavier drinkers. The tiredness and accumulated poisoning of the body cause most drinkers to feel lethargic and tired, and this state of mind is much more conducive to negative emotions than positive ones.

11.   Blackouts

Let's now consider how alcohol's effect on the limbic system
contributes to the phenomenon of blackouts. When I talk about
blackouts I am not talking about falling unconscious after drinking,
I am talking about periods of consciousness of which the drinker
has no memory. Indeed, the term 'blackout' usually has even
further connotations than this. It is usually a period in which the
drinker does things that seem completely out of character for them,
things that they bitterly regret when they emerge from the blackout.
This aspect, along with other aspects, can result in the problem
drinker feeling like they have utterly lost control, that they are going
mad or are becoming out-and-out schizophrenic. This adds to the
general feeling that they are different to other people and that there
is something inherently wrong with them. However, as with
everything else involving alcohol and addiction, there is a fairly
straightforward explanation for the phenomenon made up of the
physiological and psychological impacts of the drug. In fact, the
alcoholic blackout is made up of three elements: the immediate
effect of the alcohol; the withdrawal from the alcohol; and the effect
alcohol has on our memory. Let's now consider each of these three
elements, starting with memory.

The first point to make is that our knowledge of human memory is based on theories; it is not an exact science. We can study cause and effect and come up with theories to explain, but we cannot categorically state as fact the elements of it in the same way that we can state as fact the elements of a chemical reaction. Having said this, the most widely currently accepted theory is that human memory consists of two parts: the short-term memory and the long-term memory. Short-term memory is what we use to retain information that we do not need to retain for ever, but that we need to retain to deal with the immediate situation we are in. For example, if we are talking to someone, we need to remember what they are saying and the course of the conversation so we can react and have a meaningful interaction with them, but we have no need (usually) to recall the details of the conversation over the following years. If you think of all the conversations you've had over your life you probably won't be able to recall the detail of even a small percentage of them; however, you clearly don't forget them immediately while they are unfolding, otherwise you would be incapable of holding an intelligible conversation at all. There's no agreed time frame for a short-term memory to be retained, but most theories place it somewhere between fifteen and thirty seconds.

Long-term memory, however, contains those events that are more noteworthy and are therefore stored for longer. It is worth bearing in mind that it is thought that even long-term memories pass firstly through the short-term memory and from there into the long-term memory.

The generally accepted theory on alcohol and memory is that alcohol can prevent memories from passing from the short-term memory into the long-term memory, and that this is caused not by the degree of drunkenness on any particular occasion, but the accumulation of drinking over time. So we do not have to be blind drunk to suffer from the interference with our memory, we just need to maintain a certain level of intoxication over a certain time period. However, as with sleep, the actual science behind it is of less interest than the effect when seeking out a logical explanation for the alcohol-induced blackout phenomenon. All we really need to know from this perspective is that the effect of drinking is such that we can suffer complete memory loss on occasions when we are, in fact, very far from fully intoxicated. This is the first of the three points we have to bear in mind.

The second point is the immediate effect of the alcohol, or the actual position we are in when we are within the blackout. As stated, we do not need to be utterly intoxicated, but we do need a certain level of intoxication. This level is usually enough to rather heavily depress our inhibitions and to mess around with our emotional state (which we dealt with in the previous chapter), but it is often (unfortunately) not enough for us to drop unconscious or to cease functioning entirely. In this state we all too often do things we would otherwise be too inhibited to do and to act on emotions that have run away with us that would otherwise have faded fairly quickly. We may find something so hilarious that we cannot conceive how anyone else could fail to find it funny, or we may become so despondent that we simply have to call an ex, or we become so angry we cannot help but act on this anger. So we act in this over-emotional and uninhibited state and consequently do things that are frankly embarrassing and reprehensible. However, because of the failure to transfer memories from the short-term to the long-term memory, we have absolutely no recollection of these events when we wake up the following day.

In fact, this position is further exacerbated by the withdrawal from alcohol. As dealt with previously, when we wake up after a drink we do not return immediately to feeling normal; in fact we are more mentally frail, depressed, and vulnerable due to the after-effects of the drinking. So we are not just viewing our previous uninhibited, overly emotional actions from the point of view of normalcy, but we've actually gone even further the other way and are viewing them from an even more timid and nervous disposition. The difference between the two states is usually such that we cannot even begin to comprehend how we could have undertaken such and act, and as we have no memory of it we cannot even begin to understand our motivation. The upshot of this is that it really feels like the actions of two entirely different people.

The blackout is not something that everyone suffers from; however, virtually every drinker who has ever taken a drink has done things they regret while drinking, or suffered from some form of memory loss, and the elements described here also explain why we do things while we are drinking that we later regret, and why we suffer from memory loss. Memory loss and doing things you later regret are often seen as signs of problem drinking, whereas they are in fact absolutely unavoidable consequences for anyone who drinks regularly. If you remove your inhibitions and let your emotions run riot, how can you possibly expect to avoid doing embarrassing and shameful things?

12.   Emotional Resilience

There was a study published in the Journal of Personality and Social Psychology on 13th July 2017 that analysed the relationship between the acceptance of negative emotion and psychological health in 1,300 adults.

What the study found was that people who regularly accept their negative emotions experience fewer negative emotions and as a consequence experienced better psychological health. The study found that feelings of disappointment, sadness or resentment inflicted more damage upon people who avoided them.

The advice was simple. When you are experiencing negative emotions you should let your feelings happen and allow yourself to experience them without trying to control or change them.

If you think about it this does make sense. Take me for an example, I don't particularly enjoy conflict, and neither do I enjoy speaking in front of people. However despite this I seem to have ended up in a job which is made up of equal parts arguing (although these days it is known as 'dispute resolution') and talking in front of people.

When I started out I was terrified and got very nervous before every meeting that I knew was going to be difficult and/or attended by a large number of people. However I have done it so many times now that I am used to it, to such an extent that I don't really get nervous even if I am going into very difficult meetings with a lot of people present. If I'd never faced up to it and just got on with it however, I would never have got used to it and would still be terrified of it. If you face an unpleasant and difficult situation and get through it, you find it that much easier to get through it the next time. If you experience it regularly then it ceases to worry you and becomes the norm.

As humans our perception of what is good and bad is linked to our own experiences. For people in war zones a bad day is having their family killed, or losing limbs, or facing the actual prospect of freezing or starving to death. A good day would be a decent meal and somewhere safe to sleep for a few hours. However for most people in the western world a bad day would be something going wrong at work, an argument at home, being unable to pay bills, etc. I am not saying that these things aren't stressful but they are clearly preferable to having your legs blown off, or watching your children freeze to death. For the majority of us starvation is simply not a realistic prospect, and a meal and somewhere safe to sleep is something we just take for granted. They don't cause us to be particularly happy because they are the norm.

When I served in Iraq one of the high points for me was having a shower, putting on clean clothes, and going to sleep in an actual bed for a few hours. I was absolutely ecstatic if I could do that. However now, over ten years down the line, whilst I might enjoy doing that it wouldn't exactly be the highlight of my week.

My point is that 'good' is better than what we are used to, and 'bad' is worse than what we are used to. If you are anaesthetising the bad then you can never properly appreciate the good, which after all is just an improvement on the bad. If you are in an unpleasant situation for any length of time, such as being in prison or being in the military on active service, you eventually get used to it and very small things can make you happy. Of course it doesn't have to be anything as drastic as prison or being in a war zone, you might just be going through a bad patch with work or a relationship, or have health or housing issues, but if you are constantly anesthetising with alcohol you are never actually experiencing these negative emotions, you are never facing up to them and learning how to deal with them and becoming more resilient to them. This is what happens when we are constantly taking a drink to take the edge off our feelings whenever we experience anything negative. We are anesthetising feelings rather than facing them with the result that we never learn to deal with them.

When a person stops drinking they don't stop living, they continue to live life, with all the good and the bad. There is a very pronounced tendency in the western world to expect to be happy all the time. We see it as our basic right and if we are unhappy, even for a moment, we immediately look to remedy it, often by taking some kind of external drug like alcohol. Just bear in mind that you can be unhappy for a bit and if you are, it is not all negative. If you are unhappy or experiencing any kind of negative emotion, you are becoming more resilient and emotionally stronger because of it.

13.   Shyness – Drinking at Social Occasions

Our first experiences of alcohol often bear out the proposition that alcohol has a positive effect on us. I say 'often' because most of us start drinking when we are teenagers in social situations, such as parties and other social gatherings. While such occasions are enjoyable, they are also to some degree or another stressful. We may be meeting and talking to people we don't really know, making approaches to the opposite sex, etc. So although these situations are on the whole enjoyable, they also contain an element of stress. Some of us will find them more stressful than others, while many will find them out-and-out terrifying. Alcohol, being a depressant and an anaesthetic, suppresses this feeling of stress or fear and thus provides us with an immediate boost. However, even that benefit is actually an illusion, as no matter how shy or inhibited a person is, the psychological process in a social situation is that the feeling of stress will decline as the event progresses, with or without alcohol.

This makes perfect sense. These events are never as bad as we fear, and as the event progresses we will relax slightly and, usually, actually start to enjoy ourselves. If you don't believe this, look at how children react when they are going to a party or meeting with other children of their own age. When they first get there they won't leave their parents' sides and peek shyly from around their legs; however, when it is time to leave, they are tearing the place to pieces and it's tears and tantrums because they don't want to go. Some of us are shyer than others, some people painfully so, so it will take correspondingly longer for them to gradually relax in a social situation. However, drinking to get through such a situation actually makes things worse. If we attend social occasions without drinking then, even if we are horrendously shy and self-conscious, we will eventually relax, even if it is only an infinitesimal amount and triggered by relief when the event starts to draw to an end!

However, having got through one occasion (and I reiterate that these things are rarely as bad as we fear), when we attend the next occasion that gradual relaxing process will start slightly earlier and will progress slightly further. This is because we will have built up a bit of confidence from the last event. We will have got through it and realised that it wasn't as truly dreadful as we feared, and when we attend the next one we will be slightly more inclined to believe that it may not be dreadful, so the relaxation process will become slightly easier. Over time and by increments (no matter how gradual), our shyness and self-consciousness will diminish. However, when we rely on alcohol to carry us over our shyness, we never actually address the root of the problem as we simply rely on the alcohol to get us through. We simply reinforce the belief that without alcohol we simply cannot enjoy or even get through social occasions.

Most people will start drinking, and indeed continue drinking, to aid social occasions. Personally, I do not like social occasions. I am not, by nature, a confident or sociable person. I find making small talk difficult. Alcohol depresses nerves; therefore, it is logical to assume it would loosen you up in social situations and make them easier. However, this is just not the case. People who find conversations with strangers awkward find them equally awkward when they have been drinking. They can even be more awkward when you have been drinking as you are desperately trying not to appear intoxicated. Conversely, even when sober, conversations do become more enjoyable and/or easier after an initial awkward period. In fact, the only time I found conversations with strangers to be easy was when I had had a good few drinks, in which case I would usually end up by saying something stupid and embarrassing. So alcohol doesn't really help in a social situation, it just changes the dynamics. Instead of coming across shy and a bit awkward, you simply come across as drunk.

In fact, social situations without alcohol are invariably better. If alcohol is available, people will either drink too much or limit their intake. If they are drinking too much they will become irritating. It is very worthwhile in those situations to watch people carefully. After the first couple of drinks they will tend to relax and get more chatty. However, as they continue to drink (as any drinker worth their salt will), things tend to change. People become more argumentative, more emotionally unstable, or just plain drunk. On the other hand, in those rare situations where people aren't drinking too much and only have one or two, then, for me, it is always a relief to realise that I won't be the only one (or one of the very few) who ends up intoxicated.

Many people who have stopped drinking will find that social occasions are the times that they find it hardest to stop. This is because no matter how much we enjoy social occasions, they are to one degree or another stressful. So they tend to be occasions when we either have a conscious desire for a drink or a high number of subconscious triggers (or most likely both). These are also occasions where alcohol is usually served and is freely and readily available. This sets off the spiral of craving and pretty soon we are incapable of enjoying what should be an enjoyable occasion because we are too busy obsessing about having (or not having) a drink. We will also be incapable of relaxing and getting through the initial awkward stage because when you are worrying and obsessing about something, you are never going to sufficiently relax enough to start enjoying the event. This adds to the belief that our shyness is such that we cannot enjoy social events, and that alcohol inhibits our feelings of self-consciousness enough to allow us to enjoy ourselves. In fact, the reverse is the case. If we took alcohol out of the equation then we would eventually relax and enjoy social occasions, and this relaxing process would become easier and easier the more socialising we did.

There is actually a physiological side to this as well. Humans are social animals and are meant to socialise. When you are entirely relaxed and socialising, your brain releases certain chemicals to make you feel happy and relaxed. Again, think of children when they go to parties. They don't drink, but as soon as they settle in they are euphoric. However, the key element is that you have to be completely relaxed to get that feeling.

There are two important points to note here. Firstly, if you regularly drink at social occasions, alcohol gets the credit for this happy feeling that you would have had anyway. This is not an effect of the alcohol, it is separate and naturally occurring. This is why we feel very different going out and drinking with our friends, compared to sitting at home alone drinking.

Secondly, if you cut out alcohol and feel deprived, then when you next attend a social occasion you are not going to be fully relaxed and happy, thus you won't get the naturally occurring boost. Remember you have to be relaxed and happy for these chemicals to be released; if you are feeling miserable and deprived you won't get it. This reinforces the belief that it is alcohol that gives you this feeling, because you find you don't get it when you're not drinking.

14.   Drinking and Obesity

Given all the down sides of alcohol generally, it would seem that weight gain is, when compared to other effects, minor. However, I include a chapter on it not only to complete the picture but also because this aspect does have some implications which are further-reaching than you might initially think.

It is a medical fact that alcohol is an appetite stimulant, so if you drink you are more likely to be overweight. This results not only from the empty calories contained in alcoholic drinks, but because alcohol itself causes us to overeat by making us feel hungrier than we actually are.

However (and as ever), it is not as simple as this. Alcohol not only causes us to feel hungrier, but it also anaesthetises the triggers that tell us when we are full, which also increases the tendency to overeat.

In addition to this, alcohol can in itself be used as energy by human beings. However, unlike other forms of energy it cannot be stored as fat. Energy from food in the form of calories can be used immediately if it is needed, and stored as fat if it is not. This is why we get fat if we overeat; if we are consuming calories we do not need, they end up being stored as fat. Alcohol, however, can be used as energy but cannot be stored. You would be forgiven for thinking that this is a good thing; after all, doesn't this mean that you can drink as much as you like and never get fat from it? Unfortunately, the direct opposite is the case. Firstly, because the alcohol has to be used and cannot be stored, it means that when you are drinking you automatically have an excess of calories that must be used instead of being stored. The body does this by turning them into heat, which is why we tend to get warm when we drink. This also partly explains the burst blood vessels (giving the traditional red nose) on the face of heavy, long-term drinkers. This is caused by the veins expanding so that they get closer to the surface of the skin, where the excess heat can dissipate into the air. So the first downside of the fact that energy from alcohol cannot be stored is the very unpleasant facial changes that it causes.

The second downside is that because the body already has more calories than it needs which it cannot store, any other calories consumed from any other source will be stored as fat. So if you are drinking when you eat, virtually all the energy from the food will be stored as fat. In addition, even if you don't eat when you are drinking, every alcoholic drink contains additional sugars, which again your body will store as fat. Unless you are prepared to drink neat ethanol alcohol (which I am afraid will make you vomit and/or kill you), you cannot escape from this aspect.

Another very important point to address when looking at alcohol and obesity is the fact that alcohol causes a deficiency in certain vitamins, such as thiamin (vitamin B1), vitamin B12, folic acid, and zinc, as it actually inhibits the absorption and usage of these vital nutrients. This means we end up lacking in certain vitamins and nutrients.

Now, human bodies will trigger a feeling of hunger when (among other things) we are deficient in something our body needs. It is not just a lack of calories (or energy) that triggers hunger. We can have enough (or even an excess) of actual calories, but if we are not eating the food that contains the vitamins and minerals that our bodies need, we will still be hungry, which will cause us to continue to eat even though we do not need the calories.

So to take an example, let's assume our body is deficient in vitamin C. It is not deficient in calories in any way, shape, or form, it is merely deficient in vitamin C. So it triggers a feeling of hunger. If we consume some fruit or vegetables then we obtain the vitamin C we need, along with a very small number of excess calories, and the hunger abates. But if, on the other hand, we have a burger and orange flavoured fizzy drink, we don't get any vitamin C at all. We will certainly enjoy the orange flavoured drink, in fact it will taste like nectar to us. That is because our body is telling us that it is exactly what we need, so it tastes wonderful. But the fact of the matter is that our body only enjoys the drink because it thinks it is rich in vitamin C, but in reality it is only flavoured with a chemical, and there is no vitamin C in there at all. So we take in all the excess calories that we don't need, we still don't get the vitamin we needed in the first place, and end up still being hungry. So how do you know what your body actually needs so that you eat the right food?

In fact, you don't have to worry about this at all, for two reasons. Firstly, if you don't introduce external drugs into your system your body will tell you what foods you need by making you fancy certain foods over others when you get hungry. The second and more important reason is that a healthy human being who has a reasonably varied diet will have all the vitamins and minerals they need in ample supply. They will be able to do without the odd one or two for some fairly extended periods with virtually no ill effects at all.

So when we drink we upset our natural system of weight gain/loss in five ways.

Firstly, in the short term we introduce a drug that causes us to feel hungrier than we actually are. This not only causes us to eat more but also interferes with our deciding what food we actually need. When the body is starting to get deficient in a certain vitamin or mineral, we will usually fancy the food that contains this vitamin or mineral. This is usually something fairly healthy as healthy food is higher in vitamins and minerals. However, when we are deficient in calories we will simply fancy the most calorific food we can think of. Alcohol causes us to feel hunger for calories, so when we drink we tend to eat high-calorie junk food rather than choose healthier options, and because we are not eating the food containing the vitamins and minerals we actually need we are more likely to remain hungry even after we've eaten.

Secondly, alcohol anaesthetises the triggers that tell us when we have had enough to eat, so we are more likely and more able to overeat.

Thirdly, as the body cannot store the calories from alcohol but must burn them up (usually by turning them into heat), any other calories we consume while drinking (either the sugars in the drinks we are consuming or any actual food we eat) is far more likely to be stored as fat.

Fourthly, and as detailed above, drinking over the medium to long-term causes humans to become deficient in certain nutrients, with the result that the drinker ends up constantly hungry as the body craves those nutrients that it is deficient in. Even if we consume lots of food high in those specific nutrients, we still don't get the benefit of them as the alcohol prevents us from absorbing them and making use of them.

Finally, as drinking impacts our sleep, we end up suffering from almost constant tiredness. When your body is not properly rested it will need more energy and nutrients to compensate. The net effect of this is that we tend to suffer from an additional increased appetite as a direct result of our ever-increasing exhaustion. The other knock-on effect is that we are increasingly less inclined to exercise. Even if we are not out-and-out hung-over, the constant tiredness is a bar to exercise.

There is another aspect of this that is of particular interest to men and this is the fact that alcohol diminishes their testosterone, and a lack of testosterone leads to weight gain (which is why eunuchs are usually overweight). When you drink heavily it takes several weeks for testosterone levels to return to normal, so if you drink heavily on a fairly regular basis (such as at weekends) then your testosterone is constantly low. Low testosterone not only causes increased fat and increased breast size in men, it also leads to low sex drive, erectile difficulties, a low semen count, hair loss, loss of muscle mass, a decrease in bone density, and mood changes. This reality is certainly different to the traditional hard-drinking macho image as portrayed by icons such a James Bond. In fact, the true image of the male hard drinker is not the toned and rugged image of the Daniel Craig James Bond, but the plump, balding, breasted, weak, nervous and emotionally unstable middle aged man in a rapidly failing relationship.

When I finally stopped drinking I slimmed down to a level that I had not been at since I started drinking, and interestingly it took no effort at all. In my forties I am now more toned than I was in my twenties and thirties. I found that the ravenous hunger that I had previously encountered fairly regularly completely vanished. I still get hungry, but it is not the overpowering hunger I would experience when I was drinking. Perhaps of even more interest is that my diet changed entirely, and with no effort at all. I no longer craved takeaways regularly, and in fact many of the unhealthy foods I used to eat regularly when I was drinking simply ceased to interest me. This process, however, was not immediate, but took several months. This longer term change is due to the vitamin deficiency. It is generally accepted that it takes several months before you see the benefit when you start taking vitamins as it takes time for the levels to build up such that they have an effect. In the same way, if you suddenly allow your body to absorb and process essential nutrients that it has been prevented from absorbing for some time, it will take several months before the full extent of the benefits becomes apparent.

So far we have looked at drinking and weight gain. However, one of the anomalies of drinking is how the typical drinker is usually seen as rotund and jolly, but the alcoholic is often stick-thin and skeletal. The fact is that a few drinks will stimulate the appetite; however, the alcoholic is often incapable of eating. It is not that he or she spends all their money on drink, or that they are always too busy drinking to eat, it is that they not only entirely lose their appetite but are often incapable of eating anything at all. This doesn't make any sense when we consider it at a superficial level. After all, it is stimulants such as amphetamines that cause appetite loss and make it impossible to eat at all, and stimulants are the exact opposite of alcohol, which is a depressant.

However, when we understand the position fully it makes perfect sense. It is simply further evidence of the body's physiological reaction to alcohol. When a human being drinks at a high enough level, the stimulants countering the ever-increasing depressive effects of the alcohol are at such a level that their effect is much akin to actually imbibing a strong stimulant such as amphetamines, one of the effects of which is to prevent us from being able to eat. A drinker at this level is constantly strung out as tight as a drum skin and constantly drinking ever-increasing amounts to depress these stimulating effects, which in turn increases the stimulating physiological reaction. They are incapable of eating all but the sparsest of meals.

This is where the alcoholic journey ends if we see it through to its logical conclusion. The sensitisation and stimulation caused by the drinking is at such a level that an almost lethal dose of alcohol is required to counter it. And of course when the dose required does become lethal, that is where the journey ends.

15.   'I Shall Be as Sick as a Dog in the Morning'

It is widely known that people can become sick from drinking, usually the following day. Indeed, the term 'hangover' derives from the fact that what is experienced is a 'hangover' from the previous night's drinking. In fact, illness from alcohol is so pervasive that it is seen as a rite of passage, and if someone drinks too much and is ill it is usually either a source of mild sympathy or amusement. But if you think about it, it is really quite concerning. If someone ate so much they were physically sick, we would probably think that they had very real problems that they needed to address.

There are several issues that we need to consider here. Firstly, why would we even want to drink so much we feel sick? If you are thirsty you may crave a glass of water. If you drink a glass of water, the craving goes and so does the desire to have that glass of water.

Secondly, how can we drink so much we are ill? If you do keep drinking water despite the fact that you are no longer thirsty, you will firstly find it distasteful, then unpleasant, then repulsive. You would have to go some way beyond this before you actually started throwing it up. Your body has several failsafe mechanisms to stop you poisoning yourself. Why don't these seem to apply to alcohol?

Thirdly, why on earth should we be ill the day after drinking? To go back to the water example, if I were to drink too much water I would feel ill there and then, I wouldn't feel fine all night then feel ill from it the next morning. In fact, a night's break from drinking water would pretty much solve the problem. In the same way, if I took a poison I would feel the effects almost immediately. If you think about it logically we should feel at our worst shortly after our final drink, and we should feel progressively better as time passes. We should feel better after a night's sleep and a few hours' abstinence, not worse.

The second question (how can we drink so much we are ill?) is the easiest one to explain. Alcohol anaesthetises the receptors that trigger nausea so we are less likely to feel sick if we over-imbibe. Of course, it is possible to drink so much in an evening that you are actually sick that evening, but this is unusual and it is usually younger, inexperienced drinkers who tend to do this, or full-blown alcoholics. Interestingly, the reason they vomit during the evening is the same for both types: the amount of alcohol consumed causes an actual serious threat to the individual's life so that the nausea receptors are triggered despite the fact that they are anaesthetised. For the younger, inexperienced drinker this is because they are unused to alcohol so the smaller amounts are dangerous to them. For the alcoholic this is because they are reaching the level where the amount of alcohol required for them to reach an even keel is getting to seriously dangerous levels.

The more difficult answer to address, therefore, is the first question: why would we even want to drink too much? What is it that alcohol does to us that creates a desire to keep on drinking even when we know we ought to stop?

To answer this we could say that alcohol tastes wonderful, and as the failsafe mechanism that puts us off something if we have too much of it fails, the tendency is to just keep drinking. But again this is just too simple an explanation. We have already dealt with the taste of alcohol, but if we were drinking purely for taste we could quite easily substitute our drink with a non-alcoholic version. Besides, I like the taste of certain foods more than others. If you offered me a choice between my favourite meal and, say, my fourth favourite meal, I would of course choose my favourite meal. But if you said that my favourite meal had a poison in it that would cause me to be tired and possibly even ill all the following day, but that my fourth favourite meal contained no such poison, I would opt for the fourth favourite every time. In fact not only would I opt for it, but I would not suffer any feeling of deprivation at all and would most likely refuse my favourite even if it were the only option available.

There are also occasions when we can't get the drink we like but will drink whatever is available, even if it is something we usually claim we don't like the taste of. How many times have you been in a pub or bar when people are all drinking the same drink, which then runs out? How many times have those people stopped drinking because of this? If you have never encountered this, then I have. The former happens fairly regularly, while the latter never happens!

Another explanation which is certainly true of some occasions is that when we feel slightly nervous we often don't know what to do with our hands, so we are constantly trying to do something with them. If we have a drink in them, we are likely to be constantly sipping it. So for example, in a situation where we are standing socialising with people we may not know well (possibly business contacts) and we have a drink in our hands and nowhere to put it down, we will tend to keep sipping it. The situation is exacerbated if (as is often the case in these types of situation) the drinks are constantly being topped up. I have been in a similar situation where I have been drinking soft drinks and even when I am starting to feel sick of the drink I find I am still constantly sipping it.

However, again, this doesn't provide a full explanation. There are many situations where we are not feeling at all nervous and still tend towards over-drinking. For example, drinking with people we feel entirely comfortable with, or having a drink with someone while watching the telly, or even drinking alone. Why do we tend to drink too much in situations like that?

The fact of the matter is we keep drinking for the effect. There are two factors at play here. Firstly, that the relaxing mental effect induced by alcohol soon wears off and needs to be replaced. Secondly, the feeling doesn't just wear off leaving us feeling exactly as we did before we took the drink; it wears off leaving a corresponding feeling of anxiety, the net result of which is that we feel less relaxed than we did before taking the drink. So the tendency is to keep drinking and, as dealt with previously, the mental relaxation dissipates before the physical intoxication, with the result that to maintain a degree of alcohol-induced mental relaxation we have to become increasingly physically intoxicated.

This is the natural tendency when drinking: to drink too much. After all, we must have concluded that our mental state required chemical interference to increase our feeling of relaxation for us to take the drink in the first place. Why should we draw any different conclusion thirty minutes to an hour later, when the initial drink or two has worn off? Indeed, we must logically be more likely to take subsequent drinks because we not only have our original mental state (which we have, you will remember, concluded was not sufficiently relaxed and required chemical interference), we also then have the withdrawal from alcohol which causes us to be additionally anxious and unrelaxed.

So now we just have to deal with the final point: specifically, why do we feel ill the day after drinking and not the night we are actually imbibing the poison?

In fact, there are two reasons for this anomaly. Firstly, a human body removes alcohol from the system, metabolising it, and when it is metabolised it turns into a substance called acetaldehyde. As mentioned previously, any food or drink contaminated with the amount of acetaldehyde that a unit of alcohol produces would be banned as having an unacceptable health risk. It takes on average an hour for the body to process one unit of alcohol (a unit being approximately half a pint of beer or one small glass of wine), so it is easy to see how the acetaldehyde will build up for several hours after we stop drinking.

The second reason is that alcohol anaesthetises the receptors that trigger nausea, so it is not until this anaesthetising effect has worn off that the full extent of the nausea is felt. What we are actually doing is taking a poison that would leave us feeling extremely ill, but the anaesthetic effect of the alcohol means we can't feel the illness. It's not that we're not ill during the evening; it's just that we can't feel it!

So now we can see why it is so easy to drink too much. The receptors telling us to stop are deadened, the feeling of tranquillity quickly disperses leaving a corresponding feeling of anxiety such that more drink is required, and the full extent of illness caused by what we are drinking is not fully apparent until some hours after we have stopped. So it is really quite understandable why people tend to drink too much and can end up in quite a bad way from drinking.

However, what can still be extremely perplexing is how someone can get into a complete state from drinking, manage to stop for days, weeks, months, or even years, then still return to it. One of the things that causes the most frustration among people who work in rehab clinics is how a person can be admitted as a shaking, twitching mess, convinced they have a serious alcohol problem and determined to stop, yet just a few days later can be laughing the whole incident off and be perfectly happy to have another drink, convinced that they don't have a problem and that this time they will be able to control it. Indeed, this was my main adversary when trying to stop drinking. It was not that I couldn't stop in the short term, it was that I could never stay stopped. Over time, my desire to stop simply evaporated. For me, my drinking could be best summed up by WC Fields when he said, 'It's easy to quit drinking. I've done it a thousand times.' In the next chapter we will dissect and explain this phenomenon.

16.   Fading Affect Bias

Fading Affect Bias (FAB) essentially describes the process whereby good memories persist longer than bad ones, or more accurately, where we tend to view events in the past in a more positive light as time passes. It is not really necessary for the purposes of this book to go into the actual details and history of the research into this area; however, suffice to say it is universal (i.e. it persists the world over in all cultures and seems to be a human trait).

What FAB actually means is not that we totally forget anything bad that has happened to us and remember only the good things. It is far more intricate than that. In any given situation we find ourselves in there will be good and bad aspects to it. Some will have more good than bad and vice versa. A 'good' event is when we find ourselves in a situation where the good far outweighs the bad, a bad one where the bad elements outweigh the good. There may be some occasions that we think may be entirely good or entirely bad, but even in those extreme situations there is likely to be a mix.

What FAB refers to is the process by which, over time, our memory of any situation becomes warped, specifically as the memory of the good parts remains and the memory of the bad parts fades. More specifically, our memory of the effect on us alters. To give an example, I served in the military. Most of what I did, I didn't enjoy. I was cold, wet, tired, generally run ragged, and roundly abused. However, there was also a part of me that was proud of what I was doing. I also did parachuting in the military. I did not enjoy it. I found it absolutely terrifying. However, there was also a small part of me that recognised, even in the heart of my terror, that what I was doing was an amazing thing that most human beings would never experience. So all in all I hated it, but as ever there was a tiny redeeming feature. My last parachute jump as I write this was nearly ten years ago and looking back now I think of it as an exhilarating and fun experience. Whenever I talk of it to other people I talk of it fondly. I have to work hard to remember that I didn't enjoy it, and in fact while I remember clearly the exhilaration and relief of lying in the middle of a field having landed safely from a jump, I struggle to remember the sheer terror leading up to a jump. I struggle to remember clearly the many hours of misery spent waiting near a runway for the boarding before a jump, even though the waiting lasted many hours and the relief of landing was so brief.

Everyone should be able to relate to this tendency to look at past events through rose tinted spectacles, and even mourn events that have gone by that were less positive than we remember, or even downright unpleasant at the time. Another classic example is having children. As I write this I have two young children. This morning, from the moment we got up to the moment we dropped them off at nursery, they were screaming, crying, arguing, and generally carrying on about everything. It was not enjoyable. However, I have no doubt that in ten years' time I will be waxing lyrical about their earlier years.

This process also explains why every culture has a tendency to look fondly upon 'the good old days'. That tendency to think that days gone past were better than things are now. It fascinated me when I first learnt that even the ancient Greeks would look back on earlier periods in history with nostalgia. 'Nostalgia' itself derives from an ancient Greek word.

Again, the actual reasons for this tendency are outside the scope of this book. The generally accepted theory is that FAB helps us to deal with unpleasant situations and retain a positive outlook on life. It also allows us to maintain a positive self-image as it allows us to see the best of ourselves in past situations. Be that as it may, the fact is that FAB exists and works to make us think that earlier experiences in our life were better, or less unpleasant, than they actually were.

How this effects alcoholism, drinking generally, or any other form of drug addiction, is that over time our memory of the drink or drugs becomes warped, and warped in such a way that it seems less and less negative to us as time passes. This is as true for occasional and light drinkers as it is for heavier drinkers and the chronic alcoholic. Every drinker has good and bad memories closely related to their drinking. Over time they will look back at their drinking more positively than when they actually experienced it. This is one of the great troubles with giving anything up. The longer we do without it, the more benign or the less dreadful is our memory of being in its grip.

For the chronic alcoholic, therefore, just coming out of a particularly bad binge, he or she remembers absolutely everything. All the horror is fresh in their mind. However, in a week, a month, a year, the bad fades and the good remains. They forget how awful it actually was when they woke up in the night or in the morning, shaking and afraid, with no memory of what they did the day before. They forget how awful it felt to know the effects their drinking had on their loved ones and life. They do, however, remember the pleasant occasions when they really enjoyed a drink. Even for the lighter or more occasional drinker who has decided to stop, they very soon forget the vast majority of drinks that they took that did nothing for them, and remember the few here and there that they really enjoyed.

The practical upshot of this is that over time people tend to forget the evil and remember the benign and enjoyable aspects of drinking. Added to this is the fact that they think they have beaten it. They have gone X weeks, months, or years without a drink so have proven they can stop. If they do come a cropper they can always stop again, having already done it once. So over time the general tendency is for people to become more inclined to drink again. This is also why people can give up for some fairly lengthy periods yet still end up drinking again. It is also why there is this general belief that an alcoholic or drug addict has to hit rock bottom before they can stop. The lower people are dragged down by alcohol or any other drug, the harder it is for them to forget the misery.

FAB can alter our perception of past events, but it cannot totally change our memories of the facts of those events. An alcoholic that has lost his or her job, family, and friends and is living on the streets will not forget that. They may forget how truly awful that particular period was, but they cannot forget the fact of it, and this can be enough to keep them on the straight and narrow for the rest of their lives. To put it another way, if you meet someone and fall in love with them, then split up, you are likely to be devastated and miss them on and off for the rest of your life. However, if you marry

111

them and stay with them until you are sick to the back teeth of them, you will be more inclined to be glad to see the back of them!

The effects of FAB are even more pronounced because there are so many lovable alcoholics or heavy drinkers portrayed in film and television. Look at WC Fields, Charlie Harper, and Homer Simpson. In fact, these characters simply could not exist; the alcoholic/problem drinker is a vile, foul-tempered person, but the image remains. There are also the macho drinkers like James Bond. So when the alcoholic or problem drinker thinks back to their drinking days over time, thanks to the effect of FAB they don't see the reality, they start to see themselves in this warped and romanticised way. They start to think that it wasn't as bad as it was, and, most dangerously, they start to think that this time they can stay in control.

FAB describes a fairly long-term process, but there is another process that has a similar effect but in the much shorter term. It is nature's way that when we are feeling physically ill we also feel mentally depressed; if not chronically depressed, then certainly a lot less positive than we would otherwise feel. Again, this is just for our own protection. If any animal (including a human being) is physically ill then it should not be out hunting, fighting etc. as it is more likely to be killed. So when we are ill, the brain causes us to want to just hide away somewhere safe and rest. However, when an animal is feeling physically well the mental feeling of well-being returns, it feels positive and adventurous, and resilient. In this way the body's physical condition is closely linked to the mental.

It is also the case, as mentioned previously, that alcohol causes depression due to the chemical imbalance left in the brain after a drinking session. So when we have just woken up after a particularly heavy binge we are physically ill and therefore mentally weak, and we also have the direct depression caused by the previous drinking. We view our drinking (as we view everything else) in the worst possible light and conclude that we have a serious alcohol problem. However, after even just a day or two our physical well-being improves dramatically and our mental strength starts to improve as well. The chemical imbalance also dissipates, and so over the next few days we start to feel mentally much stronger. Things that we felt were overpowering when we first woke up suddenly don't seem so problematic. We start to get a much more positive image of the whole thing, and the chronic alcoholic self-image is replaced by the lovable drunk or macho hard drinker and in this way we become increasingly inclined to think that we do not actually have a problem, and consequently become increasingly likely to drink again.

17.   The Slowing Down of the Mind – Boredom Drinking

One of the effects of alcohol on the mind is that your brain slows down, and you end up thinking more slowly. Things take longer to process; mental problems become harder to solve. When you drink you are literally making yourself more stupid. It is this effect that leads to some people to drinking out of boredom.

On a superficial level, drinking to relieve boredom seems ridiculous. After all, boredom is a state of not having enough to mentally occupy yourself. Ordering or pouring a drink, then drinking it, then repeating this process over and over again is hardly something that is likely to keep anyone occupied for any great length of time. So clearly it is the effect of the alcohol, rather than the actual drinking of the drink, that relieves boredom, but how does it do this?

In slowing your thinking down, your mind needs less and less to occupy it. This is why drinkers can sit in a bar or pub and talk rubbish to an uninteresting stranger for hours on end, or sit in front of the TV watching rubbish that would otherwise bore them stiff. Alcohol doesn't make things interesting; it makes your mind stupid so that things that would otherwise have bored it are suddenly enough to occupy it.

This tendency is exacerbated by the general fatigue drinking causes. We have less energy and enthusiasm so can't be bothered to fill our time with a worthwhile hobby or pastime, so we gravitate towards just sitting in a bar or sitting in front of the TV. This becomes a vicious circle, with the fatigue preventing the drinker from finding something genuinely interesting with which to occupy their time, which increases their boredom, which increases the drinking, which increases the lethargy, and so it goes on.

Many people consider that they do not have an alcohol problem, yet will also say that they would rather not drink at all than just have one or two. I myself fitted into this category for many years. However, if we analyse this is detail we will see that it has some very far-reaching implications. We will explore this fully in the next chapter.

18. 'I'd Rather Have No Drinks Than Just One or Two'

My position was always that I liked drinking, that I could put up with not drinking, but that having just one or two was intolerable. I would either drink or abstain. I have also heard it time and again from drinkers too numerous to mention. It is an extremely common view shared by a large proportion of drinkers the world over. But if we look at this a little closer it should give us cause for concern. What we are really saying is, 'when I start taking this chemical substance I cannot (or at least find it difficult or problematic to) stop'. What is this if not addiction? And what is an addiction to alcohol if not alcoholism?

As we have covered previously, when we drink, the feeling of mental relaxation does not last long and needs to be replaced, so if we are starting from the position that we want a certain level of alcohol-induced relaxation during any particular occasion, we also have to accept that we are going to have to maintain a constant flow of drinks to maintain that level. However, while this provides a partial explanation as to why we would want to keep drinking when we start, it doesn't really explain why we would rather have none instead of one or two. If it was just the case that the feeling of relaxation slowly dissipated, leaving us where we were before, then

116

we would logically be better off having one or two than none. After all, if our first choice during any occasion is to spend it with a certain degree of alcohol-induced relaxation, surely if that was not an option for any reason we would be better off spending half, or a quarter, or an eighth at least of the time with that relaxation than none at all. So why would we rather have none than some?

A much fuller understanding comes when we factor in that the feeling of mental relaxation induced by alcohol doesn't just dissipate leaving us feeling as we did before, it dissipates leaving a corresponding feeling of anxiety and distress. So when we start we want to just carry on, we want to relieve the anxious feeling, not suffer it, and if we cannot relieve it we would rather not suffer it at all. So our options are drink with impunity, in which case we don't have to worry about the craving, the subconscious triggers, or the withdrawal (at least we don't have to worry about them until we eventually go to bed and wake up the following day); not drink at all, in which case we only suffer the subconscious triggers and possibly the craving; or have one or two, in which case we suffer the withdrawal from the one or two drinks we imbibe and the craving and subconscious triggers (which are much more formidable when they are triggered by the physical withdrawal). So completely logically and understandably, our options in order of preference are: drink, abstain, have one or two. Indeed, this final option is one many people simply will not even attempt.

In fact, this tendency to have none or many becomes even more pronounced as our drinking years wear on. When we drink, over time the body becomes more adept at releasing stimulants to counteract the alcohol. Some people will no doubt be thinking, 'So what, isn't that a good thing?' Caffeine is a stimulant and a cup of tea or coffee will leave us feeling more awake and energetic than we previously felt. While this is undoubtedly correct, I am sure that most people out there who drink caffeine will have had too much on the odd occasion. That feeling is decidedly unpleasant. While a small amount of caffeine will wake us up and help us to concentrate, too much will leave us twitchy, restless, unable to concentrate on anything for more than a few moments before our overexcited mind jumps to something else, and much more likely to overanalyse something and start to worry over it. What we really do when we drink is to mess with the very finely balanced chemical and physiological functioning of our body and mind, which leaves us feeling completely out of sorts.

So what is the logical conclusion? As the body becomes more proficient at countering the alcohol, it will be capable of doing so more and more efficiently. The amount of stimulant the body is able to create and release will increase, and the speed at which it does so in reaction to alcohol entering the body will also increase. So as we become more and more used to alcohol, we need more alcohol to feel normal, and the relaxing effect of a drink will wear off correspondingly quickly and will just as quickly be replaced with the feeling of worry and anxiety. Indeed, the process actually goes beyond this. Eventually the body becomes so proficient at countering the alcohol and so used to alcohol being imbibed at a certain level, that it not only reacts to alcohol that has entered our system, but it reacts in expectation of alcohol that has not yet even been imbibed. To explain this fully, by way of an example, if every time you drink you average, say, ten drinks, your body and brain will get used to this. Therefore, when you imbibe one drink your body will immediately expect the next nine, and will act in full expectation of all ten drinks rather than the one you have imbibed.

When the drinker reaches this stage, one drink will have virtually no beneficial effect at all and will leave the drinker feeling more uptight and insecure than had they not drunk at all. This is because their bodies are so used to alcohol being imbibed to a fairly high level whenever it is imbibed, that the first drink will simply send the signal that an onslaught of booze is incoming, and the reaction to that one drink will be a high flow of the stimulant designed to counteract far more than the one drink they have actually consumed, leaving the drinker feeling worse off than had they had nothing. So it is not just the case that one drink causes a feeling of relaxation that disperses, leaving a corresponding feeling of anxiety that needs continual topping up, but that for many people that one drink does nothing at all other than cause them to want several more. You start to need several drinks to obtain the feeling of relaxation and calmness that used to be obtained from one drink. This is why, as our drinking progresses, we tend to drink stronger drinks, larger measures, more quickly, or most usually a combination of all three.

It is also the case, as dealt with previously, that the pleasant feeling produced from a drink is quickly replaced with an unpleasant feeling, and another drink is required to replace it. However, this happens faster than the physical sobering-up process, with the result that the natural tendency is to end up drunk. How quickly this happens will depend on how proficient the particular body is in dealing with the alcohol; the more years we have been drinking for, the more proficient our bodies become. Of course, on occasion most individuals will be able to resist the feeling and stay sober enough to function, and indeed (on rare occasions) manage to have just one or two drinks then stop. But it will always be a case of fighting a losing battle; it will never be the natural tendency, which is to end up drunk. For the alcoholic or problem drinker it is only a matter of time before they come to, bleary eyed, with no memory of how the evening ended, and lie there worrying about what they have done or who they have upset or what new levels of degradation they have sunk to.

It is very unpleasant and disconcerting for the alcoholic or problem drinker in this position as they simply do not know why they do this, or why it is always they who seem to be the drunkest and cannot stop when they start. They understandably end up thinking that there is something inherently wrong with them. There is not. It is simply that the comforting feeling produced by each and every drink they have ever taken is replaced with a feeling of worry and apprehension which needs another drink to replace it, and this happens quicker than they can sober up. It is a straightforward physiological process and they are doing the only logical thing in the circumstances. There is a very real and logical reason why they reached for each and every drink, no matter how illogical it might have seemed to other people, or indeed to themselves at the time. Who would want to feel apprehensive, worried, and unhappy when they can feel relaxed, comforted, and satisfied? This is essentially the choice of the drinker: why they choose the drink every time, and why, if they do manage to resist it for a spell, they almost invariably end up coming a cropper again at some point.

We also need to remember that this process is present from the very first drink, but on a virtually imperceptible scale. It takes time for the body to learn to react decisively to any alcohol imbibed, and it can take some years for the effect to be fully incorporated into our conscious and unconscious minds in such a way that the addiction fully takes effect. It is also important to note that this reaction will take place in any human being who consumes alcohol. It is not the exclusive reserve of the 'alcoholic'. Indeed, an 'alcoholic' is simply someone whose body reacts in a certain, highly efficient way to alcohol and whose subconscious correctly associates the relieving of the unpleasant effects caused by the previous drinking with more drinking. This reaction is caused not by a genetic condition or flaw in the alcoholic in question, but simply by drinking over time. The heavier and more irresponsible the drinking, the quicker the process is.

These factors combined make up the reason why we often find that we exercise a real choice over whether we have the first drink, but after that the decision about whether to have another is a foregone conclusion. It is also why people tend to over-drink, and why so many people agree that they are happy drinking or not drinking, but having just one or two is not an option. It is also why, although there are many people who claim that they can have one or two drinks then stop, this will never be the natural course of action.

They will always have to exercise willpower if they want to stop drinking after one or two. The natural tendency after a drink is not to stop, but to continue.

For those who aren't sure if they fall into this category or for those who are convinced that they are not subject to the tendency, there is a simple way to test this. Because of the nature of alcohol being a depressant, and because we can neither work nor properly function while under the influence of it, and because alcohol (although it can initially act as a pick up) ultimately sends us to sleep, we tend to drink later in the day, leading up to bedtime. We therefore tend to sleep through the worst of the withdrawal and, although the withdrawal will disturb our sleep, we are not consciously aware of it.

The way to test properly whether you are subject to this tendency is to pick a free day and consume your usual amount of alcohol but make sure you have finished the usual amount by 4pm at the latest. It is essential that you do not take any further drinks after this time, and it is also essential that you do not fall asleep. It is also essential that you do not distract yourself with anything. Don't drink then head out to keep yourself busy; rather, stay in and keep distractions to a minimum. You are obviously not going to want to sit there doing nothing for five hours, but you need to be able to really see how you feel at certain intervals, without any distractions. So you could watch some telly or read, but make sure you can stop and, quietly and without any distractions, really analyse how you are feeling. See how you feel one hour after you stop, then two hours, then three, then four, then five. See whether, at the exact moment you stop up to the end of the five hours, you feel nicely relaxed with this feeling slowly dispersing leaving you feeling 100% normal and sober again. Or see if you feel an increasingly unpleasant, anxious feeling, a feeling of being out of sorts. Often this will manifest itself in a physical way, such as biting your nails or chewing the inside of your mouth or lips, or in being unable to keep your hands still.

At the five-hour point you need to be utterly alone and in a quiet and distraction-free environment. Really concentrate on how you feel. Then take another drink and make it a good-sized measure of your favourite drink. Make sure you have not eaten for a couple of hours before you drink it as this will lessen the effect. Sit there quiet and alone and drink this drink and really concentrate on how it makes you feel. See if it entirely removes that unpleasant, restless, anxious feeling and replaces it with a feeling of security and relaxation. If it does, then congratulations! You have just proven that you have the building blocks to make yourself into a chronic alcoholic!

Now let us assume you are out and drinking for a few hours. How many drinks do you think will be taken because you have a genuine choice and decide you want another, and how many do you think are being taken because that unpleasant, anxious feeling is building up and your unconscious mind is starting to tell you that you need another drink, and another drink, to get rid of that unpleasant feeling and make you feel normal again?

The five-hour period mentioned above and in the chapter on sleep is key here. While the unpleasant feeling we get when we stop drinking starts almost immediately when we finish a drink, it reaches its peak after about five hours. This can be altered if we continue to drink after eating. I would quite often drink on an empty stomach, then eat, and after eating I wouldn't drink any more (usually at this point I was too full and just wanted to sleep). On these occasions I would be wide awake almost exactly five hours after my last drink. However, if I ate and then drank some more, the time between finishing drinking and being wide awake would be much more unpredictable. This was because the human body takes longer to process solid food than a liquid. So when we eat then take a drink, a percentage of the drink gets mixed with the food and takes longer to go into our bloodstream. Therefore, although you may finish your last drink at, say, 11pm, you may not be awake exactly five hours after this as the drink (or a significant

125

percentage of it) isn't actually absorbed into our system until sometime after this. This is also why drinking on a full stomach tends to be less intoxicating; however, it is also why the effect tends to be less pleasant. Both the immediacy of the pleasant effect and the intoxication is delayed by the food. This is why so many people prefer the drinks prior to a meal to those drunk afterwards, and also why stronger drinks like port and spirits are traditionally served after eating. It is so their effects can be felt even on a full stomach.

So far in this book we have taken a very objective approach to alcohol. We have also dealt with the main effects it has on human beings, from the purely scientific to the purely psychological, and how the combination of these make up alcoholism as it is currently understood, and also why alcohol consumption is so prevalent. It is useful, however, to put this into a more subjective context and explain it further by providing some specific, generic examples. The journey to alcoholism is slightly different depending on whether an individual is a 'binge drinker' or a 'regular drinker', and by this I mean either someone who drinks in concentrated bursts followed by a period of abstinence or someone who tends to drink on a more regular, constant basis. The process is similar for both, but there are differences that make it worthwhile dealing with the two types separately.

19.   The Process for the Binge Drinker

To summarise where we are: alcohol is a poison. The constant poisoning of the body creates a general feeling of illness. The sleep deprivation will also create a generally depressed feeling (this is the case whether we drink daily or not – sleep deprivation every day will be bad, but even sleep deprivation once or twice a week will have an effect). A drink will also remove, in addition to the anxiety, the feeling of illness, because alcohol is a depressant. I stress that it removes the feeling, not the illness. In fact, although the feeling of illness is removed, the illness itself remains and is actually increased due to the additional poison being imbibed.

In addition to this, and as stated above, the alcohol causes an increase of adrenaline and other chemical stimulants to be released by the brain. This leaves us feeling anxious. Caffeine and nicotine and other chemical stimulants will also leave you feeling anxious. Alcohol, as a depressant, will remove this feeling and thus create a feeling of relaxation. That is why people who lead stressful lives, and/or who tend to smoke too much or drink a lot of caffeine, tend to drink more.

It is worth bearing in mind, however, that these effects only properly register on our subconscious mind. Our thought processes do not run as follows:

1. I feel anxious and in need of relaxation (be this due to life's ups and downs generally, the effect of previous alcoholic intake, other drugs like nicotine or caffeine, or a mixture of all three).
2. I shall have a drink.
3. That drink has relaxed me, I feel better.
4. Time having passed, I actually feel less relaxed and more on edge than before I took the drink.
5. I will now have another drink to relieve my current feeling of tension.

All we really know is that on occasion a drink makes us feel better, and sometimes it seems to have more of a positive effect than others. For binge drinkers or weekend drinkers (i.e. people who drink a lot when they drink but then take breaks from their drinking), in the early days of our drinking the negative effects we encounter after a drink are, on the whole, relatively minor and we can get through them without too much fuss. We are younger and stronger and don't have years of accumulated poisoning and sleep loss to contend with. Even when we encounter a horrendous hangover, we are only too aware that this has been caused by alcohol and it is clear to us that abstinence and time will provide the cure.

This is the real reason that 'alcoholism' as society generally defines the term takes so long to develop. Initially we recognise (both consciously and subconsciously) that alcohol is the cause of the problem. We feel sick, shaky, and depressed. We blame this, quite rightly, on the alcohol we imbibed and we avoid further drinking till we feel better. Indeed, the thought of an alcoholic drink repulses us. The conscious and subconscious mind are in agreement: alcohol caused the problem and abstinence will cure it. There is no desire to take a drink at all. Indeed, we would struggle to have a drink even if we decided we ought to have one. However, over the course of weeks, months, years, and even decades, occasions will arise when we feel ill or even not 100% right due to drinking but, although our bodies are telling us to avoid drinking, we drink anyway.

A wedding is a classic example of this, especially if the guests have to travel a long way to the wedding and have to stay overnight. They tend to arrive the day before. It is a happy, social occasion, one that traditionally includes an ample opportunity to drink, and the drinking starts. You may be seeing people you haven't seen for a while and will also probably be meeting strangers and socialising with them. This causes some apprehension, but no problem, because as soon as the socialising starts so does the drinking, we feel more relaxed, the drink flows, the whole weekend is before us, and it is an occasion to celebrate. This is a classic example of an occasion when we tend to drink too much.

The next day we will feel tired, most likely actually hung over, and our body will be compensating for the excess alcohol by dumping extra stimulants into our systems that leave us feeling additionally anxious and insecure.

Usually our reaction would be to be turned off the drink, but it is a wedding, so unless we are really bad we will end up drinking again, and probably sooner rather than later. Most weddings are early, and drinking before the ceremony is usual. Therefore, we start the day feeling less than 100% due to drink, possibly suffering from an actual hangover. Usually this would lead to a revulsion for alcohol, but the drinks are flowing and we end up being pressured into trying a drink. Providing we are not too nauseous to drink it, and assuming we are capable of both drinking it and keeping it down, the tiredness, tension, anxiety, and possible nausea and headaches disappear. This is due to the anaesthetising and depressive effect of the alcohol. We feel considerably better for having taken the drink. This may or may not register in our conscious mind, but it will certainly register in our subconscious mind. It is an important lesson that we have learnt, either consciously or subconsciously: that the unpleasant feeling caused by drinking can be alleviated by further drinking.

Let's assume this first drink takes place before the ceremony. We then sit through the ceremony. By the end of it the alcohol has worn off, but the previous ill effects the alcohol was masking have not. In fact, these ill effects have been exacerbated by the additional drink, which has caused the brain to release more stimulants. However, the problem doesn't last long, for as soon as the wedding is over we are either off to the reception or off to the pub if there is a break between the ceremony and the reception. Again we take a drink, again it makes us feel better and covers the unpleasant feeling caused by the previous drink. Again we have reinforced to our subconscious mind that although the illness has been caused by the drink, another drink will remove it. We force ourselves to ignore the part of our brain that is telling us that another drink would be repulsive and is making us feel nauseous when we smell or taste alcohol.

As we have dealt with previously, the subconscious learns through repetition. Over our drinking years, every time we drink when we are not feeling 100% due to alcohol consumption this will register on our subconscious mind. The more this happens, the more our subconscious learns the lesson and the more deeply ingrained this becomes. Eventually our instinctive, subconscious reaction when we are feeling less than 100% due to drinking changes from being repulsed at the thought of drinking to wanting a drink to get rid of the unpleasant feelings.

If we continue along this path, soon our body will stop making us feel repulsed when the idea of drinking when we are hung over enters our head. Instead our mind, both conscious and subconscious, will know that a drink will remove the unpleasant sensations, and the more hung over we are, the more we will need another drink to get rid of the hangover.

Essentially, that is what alcoholism is. It is when we get to the stage that we instinctively or subconsciously know that the ill effects of drinking can be removed by drinking more. Rather than feeling repulsed by alcohol when we have had too much, we actually start to crave it as we know it will end all the unpleasant feelings we are suffering from. The worse the ill effects, the greater our need for relief. This also explains why some drinks seem to be so essential and provide us with such a great boost, whereas others will not. The most important drinks are those when we are suffering the most from the ill effects of drinking.

I remember on one occasion I stopped for several months. I hadn't decided to stop for good, but just to have a break for a bit. When I started again I was really looking forward to a drink, but when I had one it did virtually nothing other than made me feel a bit dulled. It certainly didn't give me any particular boost. Now I realise that this was because the main boost provided by drinking is the relief of the ill effects. Having stopped for some time I had no ill effects to relieve. Had I been feeling scared or apprehensive at the time, there would have been a boost which would have been the relief of that fear or apprehension, but I was fairly content and happy at the time so there was no such boost at all.

The wedding is a fairly pronounced example of the pressure on the drinker to take a drink when both their conscious and subconscious mind are telling them not to. There is also a part of their brain that thinks that a social occasion cannot be fully enjoyed without an alcoholic drink. This, coupled with the pressure from other people for them to have a drink, means that nine times out of ten they will take that drink, receive the boost, and the lesson will impact their subconscious.

However, the situation will come up regularly on a less pronounced scale. In the UK there is a huge weekend drinking culture, and by that I mean drinking on Friday and Saturday nights. I remember times too numerous to mention from my youth when we would plan a big Friday and Saturday night and I would spend the Saturday forcing beer down my throat that I really didn't want because I was still hung over from the Friday night. Every sip of beer I managed to drink would impact my subconscious, teaching it that more drink could remove the ill effects of the previous drink. A holiday with friends was another classic example: for a week or a fortnight I would be drinking, or at least trying to drink, every day. Every drink I managed to consume was another brick in the wall that would eventually form a prison, a mental prison known as alcoholism.

In this way, and over time, alcoholism will develop in the binge drinker. The process is accelerated because the binge drinker's body and brain will get used to large amounts of alcohol being imbibed at every session, so (as dealt with previously) whenever a drink is taken, the brain will release an amount of stimulant far in excess of the first drink or two, and this is turn makes it even harder for the binge drinker to stop drinking midway through a binge; when they start, they will carry on to the bitter end. Now let us consider the process for the regular drinker.

20.   The Process for the Regular Drinker

The effect on the binge drinker as the subconscious mind becomes accustomed to the fact that a drink will relieve the ill effects of the previous drinks is quite a pronounced one. Exactly the same principle, but on a less pronounced scale, applies to the regular drinker (and by this I mean someone who tends to drink smaller amounts but more regularly). As they are drinking less, the ill effects tend to be less pronounced, so the relief they experience when they take a drink is less obvious. However, this is more than compensated for by the fact that the regularity of the relief in itself means that the process of addiction still takes effect. Whereas the binge drinker may encounter fewer occasions when they end up drinking when suffering the ill effects of drink, the regular drinker does so on an almost continuous basis.

Also, critically, the ill effects of the lack of quality sleep tend to be dramatically increased for the regular drinker, such that the 'boost' of relieving this general tiredness is more pronounced. The binge drinker who stops entirely in between binges tends to suffer less from the accumulative effects of the lack of quality sleep. Further, the binge drinker may have to wait for many weeks, months, or even years before the occasions are such that the brain starts to instinctively relate the relief of the ill effects of drinking to more

135

drinking. However, for the regular drinker, the very regularity of their drinking provides its own occasion.

Let's assume the regular drinker has only a very few alcoholic drinks, but does so on successive days. Assuming the best case, in which they have no actual nausea and/or headaches, even the very small amount they are imbibing will cause them sleep disruption, which as mentioned previously is accumulative. So, to take a hypothetical situation, on day one they have one drink. The next day they suffer very little ill effect other than a slight increase in tiredness. This could be very small indeed and may not even be consciously noticeable if they are young and otherwise have been sleeping well. However, it is there for the duration of day two, and come the evening and the next very small amount of alcohol, this tiredness is relieved. That alcohol, however, causes the next night's sleep to be disrupted, so for day three there is another slight increase in the feeling of tiredness. It is important to note that as this is an increase on day two, they have now had two nights' poor sleep, not just one, and so are more tired on day three than day two. The alcohol on the evening of day three is even more important as the feeling of tiredness that is being relieved is even more pronounced.

As you can see, as time wears on the requirement for alcohol increases as the tiredness increases. This in and of itself is bad enough, but other factors come into play. Firstly, as noted above, there is a feeling of tension and aggravation that is also caused by each drink, so that as time wears on it is not only tiredness we need to relieve with alcohol, but also that tense, nervous feeling, which has also increased. It is also important to note that, as with any poison or drug, the body becomes increasingly immune to it, so the amount we require each day increases. We may fight very hard to keep our intake at a certain level, or even to decrease it. We may even have limited and short-lived victories in this regard. However, this will never be the natural process. The natural way will be for our intake to increase as we become increasingly immune to the anaesthetising effects. As our intake increases, so do the negative effects that in turn need ever-increasing amounts of alcohol to relieve.

So, whereas the binge drinker advances with large, obvious steps that are encountered on fewer occasions, the regular drinker advances slowly but steadily. This is despite the fact that the regular drinker may not drink every single day. Just as the negative effects of sleep deprivation are accumulative, so their reversal takes time and cannot be remedied by having just one or two nights off the drink. Nor can a broken sleep pattern be repaired immediately.

Regular drinkers are even less likely than binge drinkers to stop long enough to regain their broken sleep pattern, let alone have enough further nights not drinking to start actually catching up on the lost sleep.

Now we've considered the different ways in which alcoholism can develop among the two main types of drinker, let's look at a day in the life of a chronic alcoholic. Many people are genuinely perplexed as to why the chronic alcoholic drinks the way they do, and why they are prepared to sacrifice their friends, family, job, home, and indeed their very life for another drink. However, let's now apply what we have learnt and look at things from the alcoholic's point of view to see if we can't make some sense out of it all.

21.   A Typical Alcoholic Day Explained

Let's take an average day in the life of an alcoholic or even a heavy drinker (if there is a difference between the two). We will refer to this alcoholic as 'he' as we have to refer to him as something, but 'he' could just as easily be a 'she'.

The alcoholic wakes up (or more accurately comes to) in the morning (or any other time of day). How does he feel? Absolutely awful. The poisonous effects of the drink are making him feel ill, which has the knock-on effects of making him feel weak and vulnerable, and unable to cope. If you doubt this, consider how you feel when you are ill. Do you feel full of life, confident, and raring to go? Or do you feel vulnerable and defensive? Physical well-being has a direct impact on our mental well-being. This is simply nature at work. Any animal that is ill shouldn't be going out fighting, finding a mate, hunting, or defending its territory. It needs time to recover from the illness to give it the best chance of survival. So nature ensures that that animal loses its confidence and no longer wants to do any of those things.

Our drinker is also feeling depressed, firstly from the chemical depression caused by the after-effects of his drinking, and also most certainly because by this stage his drinking will have substantially impacted his life. He will have relationship problems, health problems, employment problems, and housing problems. These things on their own would cause any healthy, confident human being to be depressed, but in his physically debilitated and chemically depressed state these things are magnified tenfold.

Added to this is the separate feeling of anxiety that alcohol creates when its initial anaesthetising effects have worn off, leaving increased anxiety. The more you drink, the more anxious you feel afterwards, and the chronic alcoholic will have consumed a huge amount and feel a correspondingly huge amount of anxiety. It is this that causes the shakes or the jitters. Again, this effect is logical if you think about it. The human mind is not designed to be in a state of constant intoxication from a chemical depressant; if it were, then the brain would be equipped with such a chemical (as it is equipped with adrenaline, endorphins, etc.) and would release it into the brain and body on a regular basis. So when we place a chemical depressant into our body the brain reacts by releasing something to counter this, a stimulant, and parts of the brain become more sensitive. The alcohol then quickly wears off and we are left with the stimulant and not the chemical depressant; thus, we are left feeling overly anxious and afraid.

So here we are with our alcoholic waking up in the morning, feeling awful and nauseous from the poisonous effects of the drink, the leftover anxiety, the sleep deprivation, and depression. For want of a better term, let us call these accumulated negative feelings 'alcohol withdrawal'. To put it bluntly, he's in a bad way. Both his conscious and subconscious mind know that if he takes a drink he will feel immediately better. Alcohol is an anaesthetic and a depressant, and it will anaesthetise the pain and curb the depression. This triggers the craving process dealt with previously. The accumulative effect of all of the above is that he is quite literally unable to function without a drink. He may fight tooth and nail, but in the end he does the only logical thing in the circumstances: he takes the drink and obtains an immediate physical and mental boost and, importantly, he also ends the craving spiral. The decidedly unpleasant feeling of tension and worry is also relieved, the depression, pain, nausea, and lethargy are anaesthetised, and suddenly he can actually function again. Of course, the effects of this drink only too quickly wear off, with the result that another drink is required, and another, and another. After all, the greater the pain, the greater the anaesthetic required to mask it. Very soon, the amount of alcohol is such that the alcoholic falls unconscious and wakes up sometime later to start the whole process over again.

The alcoholic is between the devil and the deep blue sea, or a rock and a hard place. They either abstain, in which case they are in a very bad way, mentally and physically, or they drink, and continue (and indeed exacerbate) the problem. At this stage they genuinely believe that they cannot function without alcohol, that they have some kind of physical or mental deficiency that can only be remedied with alcohol.

Falling unconscious is common and requires further elaboration in and of itself. Anyone who has encountered an alcoholic will know that they have periods of absolute unconsciousness. It is one of the inexplicable parts of the condition: the non-alcoholic simply cannot understand why an alcoholic would drink enough to fall absolutely unconscious on any given occasion, particularly if this occasion is in the middle of the day or just before an important business or social occasion. However, it is not as straightforward as it seems. When we apply the above explanation of alcohol generally it starts to become less inexplicable. Let us consider it from the alcoholic's perspective.

He is suffering from 'alcohol withdrawal'. The alcoholic is awake; in fact, sleep is probably the last thing he is capable of. Although the body and the mind are exhausted, having been deprived of proper refreshing sleep for as long as the alcoholic has been drinking, he is wide awake and incapable of sleep because of the over-sensitive mind and the considerable amount of stimulants in his system that are left over from his previous drinking. Just a few drinks can often be enough to anaesthetise the stimulants and calm the over-sensitive mind. The result is that the alcoholic can sleep again. Because they are physically and mentally exhausted, the anaesthetisation of the stimulant effects and the depressant effect of the alcohol generally cause the imbiber to fall into what, to all intents and purposes, is complete unconsciousness.

So the alcoholic is leading up to an important business or social function. He knows he must be in good form, but he is suffering from alcohol withdrawal. His conscious and unconscious mind know that a drink will remove the accumulative, decidedly unpleasant effects of the alcohol withdrawal, so the cravings start. It becomes abundantly apparent to the alcoholic that he is not going to be capable of functioning at the upcoming event without a drink or two. He also knows that he can (on occasion at least) drink vast amounts of alcohol with (he thinks) little or no ill effect. So what harm can there be in having a drink or two prior? In fact, the question is not so much what harm can there be, but how can he possibly function at the event without a few drinks? These will allow him to function at the event and everyone will be happy.

However, the simple fact is that when he has had enough to enable him to function, he has, by alcohol's very nature, drunk enough to counteract the stimulating effect that was not only causing him to feel decidedly unpleasant but was also the only thing keeping a terminally exhausted body and mind awake. He has in effect removed the only thing keeping him conscious. In this situation, the alcoholic can quite literally drop from being relatively compos mentis to completely unconscious in the space of a few minutes. It is also the case that when we drink an alcoholic drink it takes a few minutes to actually enter our system, so if the alcoholic is drinking fairly quickly (as he no doubt will be because he is in a panic to end the misery) then by the time he has enough alcohol in his system to counter the alcohol withdrawal, he has probably drunk an additional two or three drinks at least whose effects have yet to take effect. When these do take effect he has not only balanced the stimulation with the anaesthetising, but he has overcompensated.

The alcoholic is not a bad person. He is just someone who has found himself in an impossible situation and is trying to make the best decisions he can under the circumstances. Unfortunately, because of ignorance and misunderstandings about alcohol generally, he invariably makes the wrong decision, which is to keep drinking. This is not his fault, but is purely because he is not in full possession of all the facts required to make the correct decision.

22.   Do I Have a Problem? The Stages of Alcoholism

As can be seen, the process which ends up with an individual becoming an alcoholic is very subjective and is a complicated interplay between the chemical, the physiological, and the mental. There is also considerable disagreement on what an alcoholic actually is, but this is really due to society's failure to properly define the term. I always considered an alcoholic to be someone who spent every waking hour consuming as much alcohol as they possibly could, someone who could not go a single day or even a waking hour without a drink. This is one of the reasons it took me so long to acknowledge that I had a problem. I could stop; alcoholics could not. Therefore, I was not an alcoholic. I would drink for increasingly long periods, day and night, first thing in the morning, indeed whenever I happened to gain consciousness, but I didn't consider myself to be an alcoholic because I could and would regularly stop for days, weeks, even months at a time. Many people in fact consider an alcoholic to be someone who cannot stop drinking when they start. If they mean the person has a tendency or strong desire to continue when they start, then probably 80% of drinkers are alcoholic.

The definition of 'alcoholic' isn't really one we need to worry about too much. What we really need to understand is the drinking process as measured over our drinking lives: the start and end, and the major milestones on the way. When we have this in place, we will at least have some perspective on the entire process so that it becomes possible to get a rough idea of where we are. Whether you consider the alcoholic to be at 25%, 50%, or 100% of the total journey is really a question of individual preference and definition.

It is useful if we think of our drinking lives as a journey. At the start, and during our early childhood, we not only have no desire to drink but we do not even know that such a thing as an alcoholic drink exists. At the other end of the journey is the person who spends every waking hour consuming as much alcohol as they are able, to the exclusion of everything else. So an obvious place to start when thinking about our drink journey is with our first drink.

The desire to have an alcoholic drink is created in us before we actually imbibe that drink and it is created by every drinker we see, both in reality and in films, books, etc. We see people doing something and they seem to enjoy it, so we want to try it. The first drink will be different things to different people depending on the context in which it is taken. If we are in a fearful or intimidating situation (such as socialising) then that first drink may seem to be an epiphany. By depressing the feeling of fear and shyness it can change a person from a shy, timid individual to an outgoing and

146

sociable person. So to such people the first drink can make them feel that they were previously incomplete and that alcohol has completed them, and thus that they are incomplete without it. In fact this is a complete illusion; they would have ended up just as happy without the alcohol (as dealt with in the chapter on shyness), and all alcohol has done is take away a feeling of nervousness that anyone would feel to a greater or lesser degree in that situation.

On the other hand, the drink may be taken in an entirely different situation and may make a completely different impact. To take myself as an example, I took my first drink with my then best friend. There were just the two of us and I was absolutely comfortable with him. I was suffering no stress or anxiety at all; we sat together on a bench on a quiet street in Raynes Park, which is a leafy suburb on the outskirts of South West London, and drank some beer. I found the effect odd but neither pleasant nor unpleasant. It just made me feel a bit dizzy and silly. This was because I had no particularly unpleasant feelings to depress at the time, and I was not afraid or uncomfortable.

Although each person is an individual and the first drink can be taken in a myriad of different situations, they tend to fall into one of the above two categories. Either we are under some form of stress when we drink it, in which case it seems to confer an actual benefit and makes us feel like it is a part of us that has always been missing, or we are under no particular stress when we drink it, in which case we usually find our first drink to be a bit of a non-event. The key point to note is that it is not the individual, but the situation in which they find themselves when they take that first drink, that is the influencing factor.

However, interestingly, the effect of the first drink is largely irrelevant in the process itself, other than to dictate the speed at which we travel through the next few sections of the journey. If our first drink falls into the 'epiphany' category then we are more likely to drink, and drink more, on future occasions. However, for those who find their first drink to be a non-event, this doesn't mean they won't drink again. Indeed, they are just as likely to take a drink when the next occasion comes up to have one as anyone else, as very few people find the first drink to be so uninteresting or repulsive that this gives them the resolve to never take another. Most people, having tried one drink, will be just as inclined to try another on subsequent occasions, and sooner or later (usually sooner) they will take one in a stress situation, it will appear to confer an actual benefit, and this will begin to register on their subconscious.

The problem we have when dealing with this topic is, having dealt with the first drink, where do we go from here? We already know that drinking over time causes the physical withdrawal to increase as the brain becomes more proficient in countering the depressant effects of the alcohol, and that the impact on the subconscious becomes more ingrained over time, but these are gradual processes which making charting progress using this approach difficult. An attempt to use this method might look something like this:

1. Although the withdrawal from alcohol (and by this I mean the anxiety and restlessness that is left behind when the alcohol wears off) is there from the very start, it starts off being almost imperceptible. It takes time for the body to become more proficient in dealing with any alcohol we imbibe, and it takes time for the relieving of the withdrawal by drinking more to take full effect in our subconscious (the process is slightly different depending on whether an individual tends to be binge drinker or a regular drinker, as dealt with previously). Until this happens, we can pretty much take alcohol or leave it as we see fit. Although the withdrawal is there, we are largely unaware of it and don't associate it at any level with being relieved by drinking more. In fact, the opposite is the case. When we wake up having drunk the night before, we associate any illness with our previous drinking and are repulsed by the thought of drinking more. If we drink during the day and stop

for any period, we find we have absolutely no desire to drink more, and indeed we would struggle to drink more.

This is our brain working as it ought to; when we imbibe alcohol, which is a poison, and we feel the ill effects of it, our conscious and subconscious mind tell us to stop drinking it, so we do. So at this stage we may have a tendency to drink too much when we drink (as the mental intoxication is outpaced by the physical intoxication), but when we are hung over the thought of drinking more repulses us, so we stop. We may want or even crave a drink on certain occasions, but hangovers make us want to stop drinking and if we do try to 'drink through them' we find it hard work and often can't do it.

It is also a characteristic of early stage drinkers that they may wake up feeling the relaxing mental effects of the alcohol as well as the physical intoxication. Early stage drinkers often wake up feeling giggly and silly, as if they have only just finished their last drink. This is because their bodies and brains are not yet fully proficient in countering the alcohol, so the mental effects remain the following morning. Later stage drinkers, however, will wake up feeling very awake, tense, and anxious (usually in the middle of the night), and are often up at the crack of dawn and are incapable of having a lie-in the morning after drinking.

2. Over the years we will have occasions when, whilst still suffering the ill effects of the previous drinking session and finding the thought of drinking repulsive or distasteful, we will drink anyway. Every time we do this, our subconscious is learning a lesson: the ill effects of alcohol can be more effectively and quickly removed by taking another drink. Over time our subconscious reaction when we are suffering the ill effects of alcohol (and by this I am referring to the feeling of anxiety caused by a drink leaving our system as well as an actual hangover) changes from 'poison – stay away' to 'another drink will get rid of the pain'. The subconscious requires repetition, and it is only over time that this lesson is fully ingrained into the subconscious, so the longer we have been drinking for, the more deeply ingrained it becomes.

This is the main transition stage from non-alcoholic to alcoholic. Over time, and with repetition, we change from being repulsed by alcohol when we have drunk too much, to being able to drink through a hangover when we have to, to being happy to drink through a hangover, to wanting to drink when we are hung over, to having to drink when we are hung over. This is why the time frame for alcoholism is so arbitrary and can range from a few months to decades. It depends on the individual and their particular circumstances. Some people will find for many years they have no reason to drink when hung over, while others will find that their circumstances demand it from very early on. The number of times we do it is directly proportionate to how quickly we travel the alcoholic road. So in this stage we will reach the point at which we are fairly happy to have a drink when we are still suffering the ill effects of the previous drink. This is also the stage where many people find they would rather have no drinks rather than having just one or two.

At this stage our bodies are much more proficient in countering the alcohol so that we will rarely, if ever, wake up feeling the mental relaxation. In fact, we wake up feeling tense and nervous after drinking, usually at some ridiculously early hour.

3. The next stage is where we subconsciously and instinctively know that an alcoholic drink will alleviate the discomfort of the previous drink(s), and the ill effects of the previous drink cause us to want and even crave another drink. In this stage if we do for any reason take a drink when we wake up at night feeling nervous, or when we wake up first thing in the morning, we will receive a boost, and from then on every time we wake up restless in the night, or wake up feeling hung-over in the morning, we will immediately start craving a drink. If we do take these steps then we quickly move to the final stage.

4. The final stage is that of constant drinking, usually triggered by taking the morning or middle-of-the-night drink. Either way, it means that as soon as we wake up, we take a drink. This very quickly leads to the stage where the person's subconscious conditioning is such that, coupled with the craving process, they simply cannot function without a drink; indeed, they will give up everything and anything just to get another drink. This is because they believe that, miserable as life is when they are drinking, it is marginally better than when they are not drinking.

So we could break the drinking journey down into five stages (the four above plus the first drink). However, it is still vague. In fact, I think there is a far better way to chart the journey.

I once overheard a holiday conversation between three of my colleagues. One of the ladies had two children, aged 18 and 20 (clearly not 'children' but I shall use the word because 'issue' or 'offspring' sounds a bit odd). Both children were still living at home, but as you would expect they were starting to spread their wings, ready to fly the nest, and were becoming more and more independent.

What she and her husband said to their children is that they are more than welcome to go on holiday with them (which they will pay for), but equally, if they no longer want to go on holiday with their parents, then they wouldn't have to go along. I thought that fairly sensible; there is no point forcing your children to go on holiday with you if they don't want to, but equally it is very nice (if you can afford it) to keep inviting them along.

This particular year, they were going on a luxury cruise. However, neither of the two children were going along. Why? Because it was an American cruise ship, and they would apply the American age restriction on serving alcohol, which is twenty-one. So neither of them would be able to drink on board.

The conversation then centred around their decision not to go along as they wouldn't be able to drink, with everyone agreeing that it is understandable, and the mother herself taking this position. I resisted making any comment.

To put things into perspective, though, this was possibly a once-in-a-lifetime holiday, fully paid for, and the reason they wanted to stay at home was not to have the house to themselves, or arrange parties, but simply because they couldn't drink on the holiday. And these weren't two grizzled, three-bottles-of-spirits-a-day drinkers, these are two young, up-and-coming students. Of course, there may have been other influencing factors in their decision not to go (such as having the house to themselves or having a party), but the point is that it was considered perfectly reasonable for them to refuse to go on the basis that they wouldn't be able to drink.

Now I am assuming that these two 'children' do not have a problem with alcohol (or the conversation would have taken a very different turn), but it highlights the role alcohol plays in our society. It also, I think, demonstrates the age at which we become dependent on alcohol. They may not be dependent on alcohol to get out of bed in the morning or to deal with every aspect of their lives, but they are clearly dependant on alcohol to get them through certain situations, to such an extent that what should be a very enjoyable, once-in-a-lifetime experience is missed out on because the drug they need to enjoy that situation is missing.

I remember doing a similar thing when I was younger. I can't remember exactly how old I was, but it was between 14 (because I had started drinking and smoking) and 16 (as I was still at school). My parents took my sisters and I to Disney World. I absolutely loved it. In fact, there was only one occasion when I was miserable. We went to one of the few places in Disney World where you could drink alcohol (I doubt it exists anymore, it seems alcohol is now virtually unobtainable in Disney World, but this was some years ago). It was an amazing place. It was done up like an old colonial gentleman's club, but many of the exhibits moved or did odd things if you watched them long enough. My parents had told me I could have a beer when we got there, but they hadn't anticipated the far more rigid approach in the US to supplying alcohol to minors and I had to go without, so I sat there miserable all evening. I had been out every evening that holiday and enjoyed myself not drinking, but on no other night had I been promised a drink. The problem was, I was expecting to have a drink and couldn't have one. I, like my colleague's children, was at a very early stage of my drinking career, but even at that tender age there are situations where we want to drink and find we cannot enjoy ourselves if we can't.

It is usually assumed that it takes several years to become addicted to drinking; however, this is not how we should be looking at it. It is not a question of not-addicted / addicted, with a grey area in between. Rather, it is a case of becoming addicted from the start, but only in respect of a very limited number of situations (like socialising), with the later stages of being addicted applying to a far wider array of situations (like every weekend, evening, lunchtime, morning, second of consciousness, argument, setback, meal, etc). The earlier stage drinker is simply addicted to or reliant on alcohol in far fewer situations, whereas the later stage drinker is reliant on alcohol in a far greater number of situations. So I think a far more accurate way to chart the drinking journey is simply to look at which situations you would be uncomfortable not drinking at, because what this really means is that in that you cannot fully cope with, or enjoy, that situation without your drug. Even if you just think that a drink might slightly enhance a certain situation then you should beware. After all, if you are happier drinking, then you must by consequence be more miserable if you are not. This will very quickly turn into not being able to enjoy the situation at all without a drink.

So what situations would you be happier drinking in? I think the vast majority of drinkers, if not all of them, would feel uncomfortable or not as happy as they might otherwise be if they were abstaining at a social gathering with everyone else drinking. But are you also happier drinking with every evening meal? Every evening? Every lunchtime? Every weekend? Every sports match? Every setback? Every argument? Every bad day at work? Every morning to get out of bed? Every waking moment?

I think this is a far better way of considering this issue because we tend to become addicted to drinking in certain situations rather than drinking all through every day to a greater and greater degree (like we would tend to do with smoking).

However, even looking at our drinking in this way does not provide a definite guide. Many people may find that in some situations alcohol is essential, while in others it is merely preferable. As the process is so subjective and so dependent on each individual, it is impossible to be any more explicit than this. It will give some indication as to where any particular individual may currently be on their own personal journey, but it is far from a categorical guide. It is also the case that the stages can and do overlap to a large degree. Some people reading this book will consider themselves alcoholic. Some people will consider that they are not alcoholic but will consider that their drinking is becoming a problem. Often, the first questions people want answered is, do I have a problem with my drinking?

The point to bear in mind is that everyone is different. Everyone has a different view of drinking. One person's chronic alcoholic problem drinker is another person's heavy (or even average) drinker. I once heard one lady saying that she knew she was an alcoholic because she would drink a bottle of wine before going out in the evening. I would consider myself absolutely abstemious if I went out on a Saturday evening only having had one bottle of wine before I went. A friend of mine recently told me how most evenings he drinks a bottle of wine and eight cans of lager. That is the approximate equivalent of three bottles of wine, or a bottle of spirits. Some people would consider this to be chronic alcoholism, but he considered this to just be average drinking, if a little on the heavy side. The range of views not only differs between individuals, but also with each individual themselves. Our own view of our drinking is not a constant. It changes (sometimes quite dramatically) over time, as dealt with in the chapter on FAB. Sometimes we might see ourselves as a drunk and as someone who is losing the power to control their drinking. We may despise ourselves and vow to change our ways. However, on other occasions we view ourselves as someone who enjoys a drink, and occasionally might drink too much, but who (apart from teetotallers) doesn't do that on occasion?

The other problem is that, for the vast majority of people, there are always people who drink more than us (which makes us feel safe) or less than us (which tends to make us concerned that we are drinking too much). There are a huge myriad of drinkers, from my great aunt who used to have a small glass of lager shandy once a year at Christmas and make it last all day, to those people who spend every waking hour drinking at a fast and furious pace. I have to say that I have never met anyone in the latter category (although I have no doubt they must exist). As previously mentioned, Richard Burton was at one stage drinking three to four bottles of spirits a day, and yet I understand that he never considered himself to be an alcoholic.

Drinkers tend to fall into two categories. The first type tends to drink in binges. They will be utterly drunk for a few days at a time, then stop for a bit. These binges may last for hours, days, weeks, or even months (although most commonly they last for a few days or less), but the individuals concerned are obviously capable of stopping drinking for some considerable periods. They often won't believe that they have a problem because they do not drink every day. The other category is those people who drink every day, but manage to function (to some degree at least), although they may in fact consume some quite vast quantities of drink on a daily basis. People who fall into this latter category tend also to be disinclined to see themselves as having a drinking problem because they often manage to refrain from ending up falling-over drunk. They do have problems due to their drinking but, because they retain a resemblance of sobriety during their day-to-day lives, they tend not to associate these problems with their drinking.

There is no set test for alcoholism or problem drinking, and there cannot be one. Everyone must consider this issue for themselves. However, someone once said to me that if you are even asking yourself if you have a problem, then you do have one. One definition of a problem is 'a difficulty that has to be resolved or dealt with'. The fact that the question has even crossed your mind means that it is something you are dealing with, something you are seeking to solve, thus by definition it must be a problem. I believe that this is especially the case if we bear in mind that the drinkers themselves tend to want their drinking to not be a problem. We tend to ignore the warning signs for as long as we can. For the majority of people, therefore, the fact that they are finally getting to the stage where they can no longer ignore the possibility that their drinking is becoming problematic means that it is a problem, and probably has been for some time.

One point that is worth emphasising is that, when I describe the process of alcoholism as a journey that starts from the first drink, I mean that it is a journey that anyone who takes that first drink starts on. No one is alcoholic from the first drink; addiction to alcohol is usually a long process spanning many years. It is easiest to imagine it as a journey: at the start, teetotalism; at the end, chronic alcoholism.

We travel along this path at different speeds, which are dictated by our particular circumstances, such as our physical strength (which dictates how much we are capable of drinking), the circumstances in which we take our first drink (whether it is taken in a stress situation, in which case it will confer an actual benefit and can appear to be an epiphany), the drinking habits of our friends, family, and colleagues (usually in that order), the availability of alcoholic drinks (which is affected by local laws and customs as well as our ability to afford them), and our particular society's alcohol culture.

Some people, due to their particular circumstances, will start the journey and live and die before they get even a tenth of the way through it (my great aunt died in her 90s still drinking one glass of shandy a year at Christmas), while others will race through in a few years. The most obvious examples of this latter category are successful musicians and actors who are around alcoholic drinks much of the time, who can often perform while under the influence of alcohol and/or other drugs, and can freely afford them. Still others will travel part of the way at speed then slow down to a virtual halt at other stages. A classic example of this is the drinker who has got to the stage where their subconscious fully associates an alcoholic drink with the relieving of the previous ill effects of their drinking (i.e. they have the full mental make-up of the alcoholic), but who never takes the step of having that morning drink, or that drink when they wake up feeling nervous and anxious in the night, so they never actually complete the process of constant drinking. They restrict their drinking to the evenings only and

162

simply spend their days suffering the withdrawal and waiting for the evening when they can relieve it.

The final point that we need to make in this chapter is that we shouldn't just be asking ourselves the question, 'do I have a problem?' The real question should be, 'is this worth doing?' Are you getting more out of this that it is taking from you? If not, the only logical thing to do is to stop doing it. Again, let us look at it logically and objectively.

Let us take a bog-standard situation. You're stressed and unhappy, so you have a drink, and you feel better. Alcohol has given you a boost. An actual, definable, and very real benefit. You feel better than you did before the drink. But do you gain or lose, overall? The effect of the drink will wear off. Then you will be in exactly the same position you were in to begin with. The drink won't have taken your problem away, that will still be there, so you will start to worry about it again when the effect of the drink wears off. However, in addition, you have then disrupted your night's sleep, so you will have the additional physical and mental stress the following day of not having had a good night's sleep.

It is also most likely to be the case, and let's be brutally honest about this, that you are not just going to have one drink. Chances are you'll have a few, so the next day you will not only have the original problem and the additional stress of a bad night's sleep, but also, to a greater or lesser degree, an actual hangover, or at the very least the additional anxiety caused by the remaining stimulants your body has released to counteract the alcohol. So all in all, you are far worse off for having had the drink. You may have got an immediate boost, but you've paid back not only the boost but a considerable amount on top. Think of alcohol like a loan shark: someone that lends money at an exorbitant rate of interest. You will never, ever pay back less than you get. All you can ever hope for is a very short-term reprieve, after which you will be worse off than ever. You borrow £10 and you get that immediate boost of £10, but the very next day you have to pay back £20. You either just suffer having to pay back that £20 the following day or you borrow an additional £20 to pay back the £20 you owe. But then the next day you have to pay back £40. Again, you either suffer the pain of paying back that £40 or borrow again and pay back even more the following day. And so it goes on.

Hopefully, you will now have an idea of whether you consider yourself to have a problem with alcohol, and more importantly you should now have an idea of whether you still want to allow alcohol to play a part in your life. If you have decided that either you do have problem with alcohol, or that alcohol was not what you originally thought it was and are now in any way disinclined to carry on drinking, there is one further aspect you need to be aware of.

23. The Problem with Accepting That You Have a Problem

This chapter is not about the many and varied blocks people have when it comes to accepting that they have an alcohol problem. It is about the additional problems the individual encounters when we do finally admit we have a problem. To explain:

The alcohol withdrawal can leave you feeling out of sorts, vulnerable, and anxious. All in all, it leaves us prone to depression and worry. The more we've drunk, the more vulnerable and out of sorts we will feel, but the point is that while it will make us more prone to be miserable, depressed, and worried, it won't guarantee that we are miserable. Assume for the moment that you've just woken up with a terrible hangover. You've had a huge row with your spouse / partner / children / parents (or whoever you usually row with when you're drinking) but can't remember the actual details of it, you've lost your phone / keys / wallet / money, you've embarrassed yourself in front of your friends / relatives / colleagues, you've woken up in hospital / a police cell / the gutter. I've no doubt you can all factor in your own individual worst-case scenario, but you get the idea. You're already vulnerable to misery due to the chemical imbalance in your brain, and you are not mentally resilient enough to deal with even the smallest upset. The actual details of your situation are really enough to drive you over the edge. You really are going to be at an absolutely low ebb.

Now assume you have drunk exactly the same amount of alcohol and are in exactly the same physical and mental state, only this time you didn't leave the house. You wake up in bed, unadorned with bodily fluids. Not only did you not leave the house, but you were home alone, made no phone calls, no social media posts, sent no text messages, your keys, phone, and wallet are exactly where they should be, and you even have a vague recollection of taking all the empties out to a nearby local bin so you don't even have them to deal with. You have the next week off work with no social engagements, the house is clean and tidy, and you've just remembered you didn't get round to checking that lottery ticket. When you do so, you find out that you are the sole winner of the £160,000,000 jackpot. Again, you can all factor in your own best case scenario, but you get the picture. Even with the chronic hangover you are likely to be feeling fairly buoyant. I grant you, you won't be feeling as happy as you would minus the hangover, but you will be feeling significantly better than in scenario one.

What I am trying to illustrate here is that the more perceived problems you have, and the more unhappy and dissatisfied you are with life generally, the more the alcohol withdrawal is going to drag you down. Everyone is going to have their own particular reasons to be happy and their own particular reasons to be miserable. These reasons will change, not only from individual to individual, but also for each individual as time passes.

So let's now take a hypothetical person, one who does not consider themselves to have an alcohol problem or to be suffering from alcoholism in any way, but they do have a range of other perceived problems. Let's then mix in a moderately bad case of alcohol withdrawal. Just to highlight it with some figures, let's say the things that make them miserable generally amount to sixty, while the things that make them happy amount to ten, so overall they are fifty points miserable. Let's then say the alcohol withdrawal exacerbates this miserable feeling tenfold, so they are now five hundred points miserable.

However, let's now take exactly the same person with exactly the same problems etc., but this time let's pretend they have accepted that they have a problem with their drinking. So when they wake up they don't just balance out at fifty points of misery, they have far more then this because of the worry about their drinking problem. This is made up of guilt that they are still drinking, shame that they are unable to control their drinking, worry about the problem and what they can do about it, etc. So this person is not starting with fifty points of misery, but at, say, two hundred. Then multiply up for the alcohol withdrawal and you end up with a misery level of two thousand.

Of course it doesn't just work this way for people that are unhappy. You may be a fairly happy person generally, but if you have admitted to yourself that you have an alcohol problem then you are going to be miserable because of this, particularly if you are waking up (yet again) with a stinking hangover.

So if you haven't accepted that you have a problem with drinking, you wake up after drinking and just get on with things. If your life is generally fairly good then, although you may be more inclined to be miserable, you may not be miserable at all. But if you have accepted you have a problem then as soon as you wake up you not only have the withdrawal and whatever other problems you have, you also have the guilt because you ended up drinking last night, the fear that you are unable to stop, the worry about what is happening to you and why, and, more importantly, the feeling of self-disgust because you weren't strong enough to resist yet another binge. So in admitting to yourself that you have a problem, you actually create further problems for yourself if you don't then stop. This in itself causes separate issues worthy of consideration.

Firstly, it doesn't take long for the anticipation of misery the next day to permeate into the previous evening. If every time you drink you are faced with a real black depression afterwards, then quite understandably you are going to start worrying about this depression before you actually get to it, i.e. during the drinking session itself. So instead of drinking away and enjoying yourself, you are going to be constantly thinking about the misery to come and worrying about it. And what do we do when we are worried about something? Why, we take a drink, of course.

So the first point to note is that when you accept you have a problem, you are less likely to actually enjoy drinking when you are doing it, and the second point to note is that accepting you have a problem is going to cause you to drink more when you are actually drinking, which will exacerbate your misery the next day, and increases the likelihood of doing something you deeply regret, further adding to your woes the following day.

This of course leads nicely to the third point, which is that the more miserable you are the following day, the more likely you are to take another drink to relieve the misery.

Finally, people often do not just admit they have a problem to themselves, but to other people as well. In this case, the chances are that there are going to be people relying on you not to drink who are going to be upset, disappointed, or angry that you have drunk. This is going to further exacerbate your misery during and after the drinking.

You may now be wondering what my point is here. Am I now going to advise everyone to pretend they don't have an alcohol problem and just drink away? In fact, this isn't an option. While deciding if you have an alcohol problem is a personal thing and can only be answered by the individual drinker, it is not within the power of the individual to simply come to the answer that suits them. If an individual accepts or even suspects that they have a problem with their drinking, it is impossible for them to convince themselves that they don't. The factors covered here will apply regardless of whether you want them to or not. Although the question about whether any individual has an alcohol problem is subjective, the answer is not. Individuals may disagree over which particular set of behaviours count as alcoholism, but once they come within their own definition, they cannot then escape from that. Of course, their own definition may be vague, and their own position not entirely clear, but once they suspect or accept they have a problem, they cannot then resile from that.

My point is that when we stop and are drawn back to drinking, we look back on our drinking years with rose tinted spectacles thanks to Fading Affect Bias. However, what we also need to bear in mind is that the guilt-free drinking we experienced in our early years is simply not something you can just return to. Drinking evolves over time and cannot turn back to what it was. Just as it becomes increasingly impossible to moderate, it also becomes increasingly unpleasant when we are actually drinking.

This may seem a depressing thought, but as ever it is just a matter as perspective. There are many things in life we grow out of and discard as they cease to be of interest and/or use to us. I used to spend every spare moment on the PlayStation and I have very fond memories of spending hour after hour playing PlayStation games. I have still got a PlayStation, but I don't play on it as I just can't get into the games anymore. For some reason I just don't enjoy them. Maybe I no longer have the patience, or the mental agility, or the hand/eye coordination. But I don't sit around bemoaning the fact that I don't like playing PlayStation games anymore. I just don't play them and instead I fill what little spare time I have with other things, like reading, the increasingly occasional run, and getting beaten up by my young sons. In the same way, when my wife and I first got married we had a very nice two-bed house. Then we had our two boys and moved to a three-bed house. I have some very fond memories of our old house, but there is no way I'd want to move back there. It is no longer right for us.

My point is that if you have stopped drinking, don't fall into the trap of thinking you can go back to how it was. Once it sours, it sours. Once you see the defects you can never unsee them; like many things in life, you cannot turn the clock back. But this isn't a reason to be miserable; on the contrary, like any change for the better it is something to enjoy and celebrate. We will expand on this point in later chapters. For now, let's consider the disease theory of alcoholism, which states that the alcoholic has a different physical or chemical make-up to non-alcoholics.

24.   The Disease Theory of Alcoholism

The 'disease theory' of alcoholism essentially states that the
alcoholic has a different genetic make-up from non-alcoholics
which means that alcohol is highly addictive for the alcoholic, but it
is not so for the non-alcoholic. This theory has attracted quite a lot
of adherents, and on one level it seems to make a considerable
amount of sense. It explains why some people can seemingly take
alcohol or leave it, whereas others simply cannot seem to leave it
alone.

It also explains why some people seem to come from a long line of
alcoholics. Perhaps most importantly, it also explains why an
alcoholic who has stopped drinking can never take another drink,
and if they do so they do not at that point start drinking normally,
but precipitate straight back to their previous problem drinking.
After all, such drinkers can have stopped drinking for many years
or even decades. They can have no alcohol left in their system and
they must be over any physical withdrawal. In theory they should
be able to take up drinking as if they had never drunk and drink
sensibly within specifically defined parameters, yet all too often they
are incapable of doing so.

The Big Book (the primary text of Alcoholics Anonymous) tells a story of a young up-and-coming businessman who worked out that his drinking was a problem and was interfering with his work, so decided to give up but on the condition that he would start again when he retired. He subsequently did so and ended up dead from chronic alcoholism within three months. All in all, therefore, there is some considerable evidence to support this disease theory of alcoholism. However (and as with so many other aspects of alcohol and alcoholism), an even cursory analysis blows this theory completely out of the water.

Firstly and most importantly, it is agreed that alcoholism is a disease of gradual onset. Indeed, this is one of the very few generally accepted 'facts' about alcoholism that is borne out by the actual situation. The scientific texts confirm that it can take anywhere from between two and twenty years for alcoholism to develop, with a figure in the early teens being the average. This is because it takes time for the mental triggers to be fully ingrained in the subconscious. No one has ever taken one drink and from that second been compelled to drink all day every day until their death. There is a period of drinking over several years during which alcoholism develops.

This simple fact alone completely negates the disease theory. If a person does indeed have a genetic make-up that means that alcohol is highly addictive for them, how can it possibly be that the addiction doesn't take hold immediately? How can it be that they can drink for several years and still be in the range of 'normal' drinking? It helps to put it in perspective by considering something that is widely accepted to be highly physically addictive, such as heroin. Is it in any way conceivable that someone could imbibe heroin on a regular, daily basis for several years yet still not be addicted to it? If they could, then either heroin would not be addictive, or that person would be considered to have some genetic mutation which meant that heroin was simply not addictive for them. How then can it be considered that this genetic alcoholic, who is supposedly destined from birth to be in a state where they become highly addicted to alcohol, can in actual fact imbibe alcohol over several decades without becoming addicted to it? It simply does not make sense.

In fact, all the other aspects that would seem to support the disease theory of alcoholism can quite easily be explained in other ways. This book explains how alcoholism takes effect; it is purely down to the long-term consumption of alcohol, its physical effects on the body, the subconscious triggers, and the mental craving. This is why some people can take it or leave it and yet others show classic symptoms of being addicted to it.

The fact that many alcoholics seem to come from a long line of alcoholics and/or heavy drinkers is also easily explained without recourse to the disease theory. If you are brought up in a culture where heavy drinking is the norm and alcohol is freely available, you are more likely to drink heavily yourself and in time are more likely to develop alcoholism. If you are brought up in an environment that has caused previous family members to travel the path of alcoholism at a quick pace, it is likely that these same factors will equally affect you.

Finally, and very importantly, we come to the point about ex-alcoholics who may have stopped for many years, or even decades, being incapable of ever drinking normally again. As we have covered, alcoholism is essentially a mental state where the mind, when confronted with any form of physical and/or mental stress (including hunger, hangovers, guilt, the very slight physical aggravation caused by imbibing one drink, the often very minor stresses and strains of everyday life that most of us take in our stride, and even the mental stress of wanting an alcoholic drink when we have vowed not to have another), will react by triggering a desire for an alcoholic drink. This is because it has, over many years, come to associate the imbibing of an alcoholic drink with the relief of this physical and/or mental stress. This in turn creates the craving spiral discussed previously.

Now let us look in detail at our non-drinking alcoholic, the person who has stopped for many years and is now going to recommence drinking on the assumption that they can return to 'normal' drinking (whatever that may be). Let's assume he or she was an alcoholic (i.e. they have the above mental reaction to any physical and/or mental stress). Let us also assume that they have stopped drinking entirely for, say, twenty years. However, let us also assume that they have made a decision to drink again in the belief that, having had no alcohol for twenty years, they have effectively cured their alcoholism and will now be able to drink normally.

The problem is that what has been learnt can never be unlearnt. The mental state of alcoholism is created when the subconscious mind instinctively knows that the one cure for the ill effects of alcohol (and by this I mean every ill effect, from the minor physical aggravation created by one drink right up to the chronic hangover or the depression caused by long-term heavy drinking) is more alcohol. This remains even if we have stopped for many years. So any drink will automatically cause the desire for the next, and this applies for the rest of the alcoholic's life. An alcoholic is really just someone who knows more about the effects of alcohol on both a conscious and subconscious level than a non-alcoholic. The alcoholic knows, subconsciously, that the ill effects of drink can be relieved by another drink; the non-alcoholic does not. So when the alcoholic starts to suffer from the ill effects of alcohol leaving their system, the old thought processes are very soon reawakened and in no time at all they end up right back where they started when they stopped drinking. The alcoholic knows on a conscious and subconscious level that a drink will remove the ill effects of the previous drinks, be that an actual hangover or the less pronounced feeling of anxiety that is caused by the alcohol of a single drink leaving their system. They won't forget this after a year, after ten years, or even after a hundred years!

So our non-drinking, re-drinking alcoholic takes a drink. The old mental triggers remain. What happens? Well, only two things can happen. They either precipitate right back to where they were when they stopped drinking, or they resist the next drink. However, even if they do resist, then they will still end up back where they started. Remember that they haven't taken that one drink on the basis that they will have one and then never have another. They have taken it on the basis that they will start drinking 'normally' again. So if they do manage to resist that second drink, then in a few days, weeks, or whatever, when they next want a drink, they can quite legitimately say that their last drink didn't lead to a huge binge, that they were able to have just that one drink, so they are safe now to have another one. They have been cured; why else could they have had one drink and then stopped?

On that occasion as well they may end up having only one or two drinks, but this only makes them even more likely to have a drink the next time they fancy one. The more they resist, the more they become lulled into a false sense of security and the more likely they are to eventually trip up. As the mental triggers still remain, no matter how long they have stopped for, it is only a matter of time before they end up right where they were when they stopped drinking. Their mind has learnt, many years before, through constant repetition, that another drink will alleviate that unpleasant feeling. It has learnt that and it will never be forgotten. They are not in the position of someone who has never drunk, whose mind simply would not be able to conclude on a subconscious level that another alcoholic drink will alleviate that unpleasant feeling. Their mind will remember the lesson, and even after twenty, thirty, or even forty years it will still remember, and if they have a drink ever again their mind will set in motion a craving for alcohol.

If we go back to the comparison between alcoholism and a journey along a road, the best analogy for stopping for a considerable period is not that we then start again from the beginning. It is more accurate to say that we just rest by the side of the road, and if we start again we then go back to the exact spot we were when we stopped. Another way of looking at it would be to say that we do indeed start again from the beginning but, having already travelled many of the different parts of this particular road, we are familiar with them and therefore travel them much faster than the first time round, to such an extent that parts that could have taken us decades to travel the first time round can be covered in days or even hours the second time round.

One of the most influential proponents of the disease theory of alcoholism is Alcoholics Anonymous, and indeed they are such a well known entity in the world of alcoholism that is it worth our considering the organisation and their methods for stopping drinking in some detail.

25.   Alcoholics Anonymous

AA is the main organisation for the recovery of alcoholics. It is a 12-step programme, the steps being:

1. We admitted we were powerless over alcohol—that our lives had become unmanageable.
2. Came to believe that a power greater than ourselves could restore us to sanity.
3. Made a decision to turn our will and our lives over to the care of God as we understood Him.
4. Made a searching and fearless moral inventory of ourselves.
5. Admitted to God, to ourselves, and to another human being the exact nature of our wrongs.
6. Were entirely ready to have God remove all these defects of character.
7. Humbly asked Him to remove our shortcomings.
8. Made a list of all persons we had harmed, and became willing to make amends to them all.
9. Made direct amends to such people wherever possible, except when to do so would injure them or others.
10. Continued to take personal inventory, and when we were wrong, promptly admitted it.

11. Sought through prayer and meditation to improve our conscious contact with God as we understood Him, praying only for knowledge of His will for us and the power to carry that out.
12. Having had a spiritual awakening as the result of these steps, we tried to carry this message to alcoholics, and to practice these principles in all our affairs.

Essentially, what the AA programme consists of is accepting that you have a problem, seeking help from God, then making amends for any wrongdoing. Obviously it is a bit more complicated than that, but these are the main points. It is very much open to debate how effective it is. It is anonymous, therefore no records are kept, so keeping track of those who manage to stop for good is very difficult. However, it does work for some individuals, be it in the short or long term.

One of the reasons that Alcoholics Anonymous works for some people is this fundamental aspect of giving everything over to God (or a higher power). Essentially what we are saying is, 'here is my life. I have made a mess of it, you take it and guide me'. It works so well for so many people because it breaks the spiral of craving that is the backbone of any addiction. It allows the alcoholic to effectively remove themselves entirely from this craving process. One moment they are in full swing in the craving process, but if they can hand everything over to God, i.e. abandon the entire craving process, they immediately gain relief and the craving, in effect, disappears. When the spiral of craving starts it can be very overpowering, but it is entirely mental (albeit that it is usually triggered by physical feelings of stress or anxiety), and indeed this is what defeats most people when attempting to quit anything, or even when attempting to diet. By 'turning everything over to God' you can effectively end the spiral, provided it is done correctly.

Let's assume an individual is right in the middle of a really bad spiral of craving and is just about to cave in. Suddenly he 'turns everything over to God'. He effectively stops thinking about having a drink, fantasising about how it would taste and how it would make him feel, thinking about how miserable he is without one, wondering how he can ever be happy again, and feeling deprived and miserable. He has emptied his mind of all that and, surprise surprise, the craving has gone.

Exactly the same principle applies to faith healers who profess to cure addiction. And of course for the AA adherent, having done it once, their confidence is built up, the person really starts to believe, and each time it happens it becomes easier and easier and more and more effective. And of course, as you stop poisoning your body, your physical health recovers and so does that feeling of confidence and happiness that accompanies physical well-being. This also enforces the feeling that there is something new and wonderful within you and the adherent to AA puts this down to God; the new feeling of physical well-being, along with the accompanying feeling of mental strength and happiness (caused in part by the return to physical health and in part by the feeling of confidence created by finally defeating alcoholism and finding a way to solve a problem that the alcoholic previously thought was unsolvable and fatal), is put down to a higher power entering the person's soul.

It is a fine system as long as it works but, being based on a fallacy, it is all too easy for it to go wrong. Everyone has bad days on occasion, be they drinkers, non-drinkers, or ex-drinkers, and when those sorts of days come along, the AA convert can feel they have been abandoned by God or sense that something has gone awry, and suddenly the whole thing can collapse like a house of cards. There is of course more to the AA than this – it also provides a network of individuals that the person can turn to, and meeting with others in a similar situation also helps the individual through the bad times. So between the network, the meetings, and the mental exercise designed to cut the craving process dead, AA provides a fairly good way of quitting drinking.

The problem with AA is twofold. Firstly, it is one of those systems that is only effective when you believe in it. As I say, once doubt starts to creep in (as it all too often does), the whole thing can crumble. As soon as any doubt creeps in, the cycle of craving is not broken. If we are in the middle of a craving spiral and we decide to hand everything over to God, but we have doubts as to whether this will work, we don't completely empty our mind. Part of our mind is thinking about whether the craving has gone and about whether we still want a drink, which perpetuates the spiral. So it is good while it works, but it is flimsy, it very easily breaks down, and just as it becomes stronger each time we successfully use it, so it becomes progressively harder to use it successfully again when doubt starts to creep in. If we are expecting or even suspecting it will fail then, again, we are still thinking about the drink and whether we want one, which perpetuates the craving spiral.

Secondly, AA advocates the disease theory of alcoholism. The reason it does this is because it provides an effective reason why the alcoholic can never have another drink: you are an alcoholic, you are different to other people, you can never have another drink, not even one, and if you do you will immediately degenerate into alcoholism.

In fact, as discussed above, the ex-alcoholic can never have another drink, but not because they are genetically different from non-alcoholics. Rather, this is because once their subconscious and conscious brain has learnt that the ill effects of alcohol can be relieved with more alcohol, this can never be unlearnt. If they ever take a drink again, their brain will trigger a desire for another drink and, as the effect of that drink wears off, so the craving will start again.

While the disease theory of alcoholism is good as it provides a valid reason not to take a single drink, it also has a corresponding and extremely dangerous and damaging downside in that it perpetuates the idea that if you are not a genetic alcoholic you must be able to drink with impunity, safe in the knowledge that you will never develop a problem. It is this belief that causes so many people to become an alcoholic in the first place. AA, in perpetuating the disease theory of alcoholism, may help some people escape from alcoholism (either in the short or long term), but it encourages so many more people to become an alcoholic in the first place. In our early years we show no signs of alcoholism, we have no fear that we are alcoholic, so we have no reason to limit or to be careful of our drinking; in fact, it provides licence for us to drink as irresponsibly as we like. However, when we do this then we speed up our journey towards alcoholism. This is the main view that society needs to change, the main fact that it must accept, if it is ever to start to win the war against alcoholism: that any person who drinks too much or drinks irresponsibly over a period of time will end up an alcoholic. No one is safe.

26.   Just One Drink

One of the reasons AA advocates the disease theory of alcoholism is that it provides a reason why the alcoholic can never have another drink. Not one. If they do, they will end up right where they were when they stopped. This doctrine of resisting just one drink is key to the programme, and the idea is that you only have to resist one drink: the first one. If you don't have the first one, then you can't have the second and you have stopped drinking. This may seem too obvious to need to state. However, the reasoning behind it is quite intricate and worth considering in detail.

Many heavy drinkers or alcoholics spend many years trying to drink the right amount. Many have a magic number, say four drinks, that will leave them feeling relaxed and happy, but won't have the damaging side effects like unconsciousness, violence, arguments, job loss, breakdown of personal relationships, etc. Indeed, it is a system that is often supported and advocated by their friends and relatives. When alcohol problems first become apparent, the drinker is usually encouraged to control it rather than to abstain entirely. They work hard to beat the system by drinking just the right amount. Superficially, it seems to make sense. However, when we understand the facts behind alcohol, it is quite clear that this cannot work.

Firstly, and most obviously, alcohol does not remain in our system forever. It leaves. If we have formed the view that one drink, or two, or four, or whatever, leaves us at our best, we must also acknowledge that when the alcohol from those optimum number of drinks leaves our system we will need more to replace it. So even on a superficial level, the solution of limiting the amount we drink is ridiculously difficult. We would be forever trying to calculate exactly when we would have to drink the next drink so that the level remained constant.

However, if we then take into account the actual facts about alcohol, we can see that the system is even more flawed. Firstly, we need to remember that the body counters the relaxing effects of the drink so that when those drinks wear off the body's physiological reaction will be that we will feel irritable, restless, and unhappy without a further drink. If we also consider that the intoxication process and the feeling of relaxation don't progress at an equal pace, and that the unhappiness surfaces at a quicker rate than we sober up, we see that this system cannot possibly work. If four drinks provide us with our optimum mental well-being, the mental well-being will tail off before we sober up, so we need more drinks to keep the mental well-being, but these additional drinks (along with the effects of the previous drinks) will cause us to end up absolutely intoxicated. In fact, this is exactly what does happen.

The fact is that the vast majority of drinkers only exercise genuine choice over their first drink. If you cannot resist the first drink, you have no hope of resisting the subsequent drinks. If you have made the decision that x, y, and z has happened in your life and you need a drink, then after a drink you not only still have x, y, and z, but also the additional problem that you now have the physical withdrawal from alcohol and the associated craving for another drink. If you can't resist a drink after x, y, and z has happened, how on earth can you possibly expect to resist a drink if you have x, y, z, and the additional physical withdrawal and associated craving?

The other issue, of course, is that having a drink breaks down any barrier we may have built up against drinking. The same is true of smoking or any other drug addiction, or even breaking a diet. When the chronic alcoholic who doesn't fully understand alcohol stops drinking, they have a huge battle on their hands. They have physical and mental suffering ahead, most of which could be (momentarily at least) relieved by taking a drink. They also have the constant mental triggers and the associated cravings to deal with.

The only way that they can resist a drink under these circumstances is to build a mental wall, a ring of defences if you like, to protect them from the temptation. This can take many forms: it is usually negative (by concentrating on the ill effects of their drinking), but it can also be positive (by looking forward to the gradual improvement in their life as their years of drinking and the effects of this are left behind), or a mixture of the two. This wall can take many forms and is not static, but is essentially made up of all the reasons that prevent them from taking a drink. The strength of this wall will ultimately dictate if they are successful or not. As soon as they take a drink, they are tearing down that wall. Their defence against a drink has been demolished, it has gone.

Logically, if we are capable of building a wall that is strong enough to protect us against drinking any drink, then we should be capable of building a wall that will protect us from most but not all drinks, as this second task would seem to be easier. After all, if we were asked to design a prison which would prevent 90% of the people incarcerated there from escaping, this would logically appear to be an easier task than designing a prison which was escape-proof, i.e. not one single person would be capable of escaping from it. However, this is not how it works; if it did, then anyone who was able to stop drinking for any short period would be capable of controlling their drinking. The fact is that if we cannot resist drink number one, we are not going to be able to resist drink number two, or three, or four, etc. We can either resist a drink, or we can't. And if we can't, then we precipitate back to square one.

Often, when we try to stop drinking, the wall simply isn't strong enough to resist temptation. This is where we give in to the craving. However, even if the wall is strong enough to begin with, the effects as dealt with in the chapter on FAB mean it weakens over time as our memory of the bad parts of life when we were drinking fade. Some people also tear it down themselves in the mistaken belief that it has served its purpose, that having had the power to stop drinking they now also have the power to control it.

In the UK there is a saying: you are just as well hanged for a sheep as a lamb. It harks back to the days when stealing was punishable by hanging. What it is really saying is that if you are caught you'll be hung either way, so you may as well steal the larger sheep then the smaller lamb. There is a similar saying in Iran that, if you are drowning, it doesn't matter if you are a few inches underwater or several fathoms. What it really amounts to is that when we cross a line, we cross it. With any form of drug addiction there is no halfway house: we either imbibe a drug or we don't. If we do imbibe it then we haven't stopped.

On one occasion I stopped drinking for some four months, and then started drinking again. When I had that first drink, two things happened. That small cloud that had been hovering over me for four months (that something was missing from my life as I had stopped drinking) disappeared. Secondly, the physical effects of the alcohol kicked in. The depressants made me feel more relaxed; the cloud had finally gone. Counteracting this, however, was a larger cloud, one that was caused by the fact that I had started drinking again, and while I hoped that this time I would be able to control it I knew, or at least suspected and feared, that this would not be the case.

My body then counteracted the alcohol by releasing stimulants, and as the alcohol wore off I felt slightly empty and insecure, and I knew (subconsciously if not consciously), from all the thousands of other drinks I had taken over the years, that another drink would remove that insecure feeling and leave me feeling content, safe, and relaxed.

So I had a few drinks, but I was still hoping that this time I would be able to control things, so I stopped after a few and went home. The alcohol wore off, leaving the excess of stimulants, which in turn caused me to feel empty and insecure. I didn't sleep properly and the next day felt well under 100%, not so much from the physical hangover, as I didn't have that much to drink, but the lack of proper sleep and the leftover stimulants still in my body.

At that point I knew, from previous experiences over many years, that a drink would take away this unpleasant feeling. This knowledge was both conscious and subconscious. When this is known it cannot be unknown, we cannot simply forget it.

The fact is that one drink is fatal, and that there is no return to normal drinking. This is not due to the fact that the alcoholic is genetically different to the non-alcoholic, but because he or she will always remember that the ill effects of drinking can be relieved by yet more drinking.

So far we have looked in some detail at alcohol and what happens when human beings imbibe it. Let's now look at it from the other side and consider what happens when they don't; specifically, what happens when a long-term drinker stops and why it can be so difficult for them to stop (and when I say stop I mean stop, absolutely and forever, as opposed to just pausing for a bit).

27. Stopping Cold Turkey – The Physical

When I refer to stopping cold turkey, what I am referring to is stopping with no understanding of how alcohol actually works, so in effect anyone stopping without the use of this book. In this chapter we will concentrate on why it is so difficult to stop in these circumstances and we can then, in the next chapter, look at how we can avoid the difficulties and make stopping as easy as possible.

The best way for us to do this is to take the chronic alcoholic as an example, as this will give us the worst-case scenario. Anyone contemplating stopping will then know that this is the worst they can expect, whereas if they are in any way short of being a full-blown alcoholic they can expect a correspondingly easier time of it.

Let's deal with the physical side of it first. This time our imaginary alcoholic can be female. When she stops drinking, the alcohol will quickly start to leave her system, leaving behind it the over-sensitive mind, the stimulants, and the depression. In addition, as the anaesthetising effect of the alcohol wears off, the true sense of the physical dilapidation will be felt, which will include the nausea and illness caused by the previous drinking. When our drinker gets to five hours after the last drink, this will peak. The stimulants will be such that she will be completely unable to sleep, but will also leave her mind in such a flutter that she will be unable to concentrate on anything for long enough to take her mind off her misery. If she tries to watch a film or read a book, she will be unable to concentrate on it. The stimulants and nausea will also make it impossible for her to eat or drink anything (and in this context I mean a non-alcoholic drink). This is a very unpleasant period, but fortunately it only lasts for twenty-four hours.

After twenty-four hours the ex-drinker will still be in a bad way and rather shaky, but she will start to be able to eat and drink (non-alcoholic drinks of course); indeed, she will find her appetite starts to return and she will begin to experience thirst again. However, residual stimulants will still remain, so she will find she can eat a lot less than she previously could, and what she does eat will make her feel much fuller than it ordinarily would. She will also start to feel tired and will be able, that night, to get some sleep. However, this night's sleep (her second after stopping drinking) will be extremely broken and unrestful and she will likely find herself plagued by dreams so vivid that they are more akin to hallucinations. However, as opposed to night one, there will at least be some sleep.

One thing that can happen during the first 6–48 hours after drinking is what's known as 'alcohol-induced seizures'. Many people know about these, and those that do will also tell you that they are caused when stopping drinking, that they can be fatal, and that the conclusion therefore is that, for chronic long-term alcoholics, stopping drinking suddenly can be fatal. However, once again the scientific studies demonstrate that these perceived 'facts' have little basis in reality.

These seizures are essentially epileptic seizures. Epilepsy is three times higher among alcohol-dependent people than among the general population. However, the prevalence of alcoholism among people with epilepsy is virtually the same as among the general population. The conclusion is that alcoholism causes epilepsy, or at the very least it increases the severity of it so that borderline epileptics suffer much more pronounced symptoms when they drink. Indeed, alcoholism can mean the difference between suffering seizures and not suffering them. Things that increase the chances of epileptics suffering from seizures are fatigue, malnutrition, lack of sleep or rest, hypertension, stress, diabetes, and blood sugar imbalances. All of these are symptoms of long-term heavy drinking.

With regard to these seizures being fatal, there are no properly documented cases showing death caused by the seizures. In every case, other causes can explain the death. It is worth remembering that the chronic alcoholic is physically extremely debilitated and often stopped drinking because they have drunk so much their body is already shutting down.

Having said this, there is considerable evidence that stopping drinking suddenly can be fatal, although this is usually caused by delirium tremens. Delirium tremens is different to the dreams/hallucinations referred to above; it is much more serious but tends to occur among only the very heaviest long-term alcoholics, commonly affects those who have been alcoholics for more than 10 years, and it is estimated that only 5% of alcoholics will suffer from delirium tremens. However, rare it may be, but trivial it most certainly is not. If you do make the decision after reading this book that you wish to stop drinking, you should seek medical advice before doing so. Your doctor will be able to advise you whether you ought to be monitored when stopping.

Let's assume, however, that our imaginary alcoholic doesn't suffer from delirium tremens or seizures. What she will find is that she will feel progressively better as the days progress, and her sleep will become progressively better. She will be tired during the day (due mainly to the lack of sleep), but this also will lessen as her sleeping improves. She may wake up sweating profusely at night, but this is an excellent sign. The body sweats for many reasons, but one of these is to rid itself of toxins. The night sweats are the body ridding itself not only of the alcohol and associated toxins, but also the remaining stimulants released to combat the depressive effects of the alcohol. By the fourth or fifth day she will be virtually back to normal physically, and by this I mean the actual physical withdrawal (specifically the stimulants and over-sensitive mind) will be entirely gone. The alcohol will have left her system, as will the chemical after-effects. She will still not physically be 100% in comparison to never having drunk, as it will take time for her to fully catch up on the lost sleep and lost nutrients. However, providing she is otherwise sleeping well, she will have caught up on 90% of the lost sleep by day fourteen. The lost nutrients aspect takes a bit longer to be remedied: around three months, providing she is eating a healthy and varied diet.

And that is it. The dreaded alcohol withdrawal process. Day and night one is bad. Day two is bad but better. Days three to five aren't perfect, but you will be well and truly over the worst of it physically, and by day five the physical withdrawal, even in the worst cases, is done with. However, for several months going forward you will continue to gain many substantial benefits as nutrients are replaced and the full effect of sleeping properly is felt. It is also worth bearing in mind that this only applies to the very heaviest drinkers. For those who don't drink all the time, or tend to drink slightly less, these first few days won't be much different from any other time or getting through any other hangover.

But it can't be as simple as this, can it? What about the drinkers who are still craving a drink after weeks, months, years, or even decades? The physical withdrawal is over in five days. Period. When anyone craves alcohol after five days, this craving is triggered by the mental instead of the physical. We will consider this in the next chapter.

28.   Stopping Cold Turkey – The Psychological

We have already dealt with two of the psychological bars to
stopping: the subconscious triggers and the spiral of craving. The
subconscious triggers a desire for a drink not only when a drinker
suffers the chemical withdrawal from alcohol, but whenever the
person in question suffers any stress or anxiety at all. The stress
from the withdrawal is very similar to the stresses and strain of
everyday life. So just because the physical withdrawal has ended,
the mental associations continue and, as we have discussed
previously, the subconscious triggers will set in motion the spiral of
craving, which is one of the mainsprings of addiction. So the mental
addiction will always outlive the physical addiction.

With the subconscious triggers and the spiral of craving it is
impossible to put a time frame on it and it can last forever. Every
time you start fantasising about having a drink, you start a craving.
This is the bad news. The other bad news is that as time passes
FAB takes effect, so on the one hand the craving can continue and
on the other hand the fear of drinking that triggered the attempt to
stop in the first place is diminishing. Were my drinking years really
that bad? Was I an alcoholic or just a lovable rogue who tended to
drink too much? Surely this time I can control my intake? The

combination of these factors is why, for many people, the longer they stop for the more likely they are to start drinking again.

However, let's now look at the good news. When I say that the subconscious triggers and spiral of craving 'can' last forever, in practice they rarely do. Even in the worst-case scenario where a person is utterly miserable without a drink on a certain occasion, if they can get through that occasion then they have built up their confidence ever so slightly. It is also the case that in, say, a social situation, it is unlikely that we can crave incessantly. Sooner or later someone will talk to us and we'll have to respond, or we will be given food and we start to enjoy it, or a myriad of other things will happen that take our concentration. When this happens and our mind becomes occupied with something else, we entirely short-circuit the craving spiral. For this period, no matter how short, we have been able to function normally, even to the extent of actually enjoying ourselves, or at the very least by not being acutely miserable!

These periods, no matter how brief and rare, will happen, and when they do, by very small increments, we start to build up confidence in our ability to cope without a drink. The craving is worst when we cannot envisage how we can cope in a certain situation without a drink. When we have got through such a

203

situation without a drink, and if for a brief period we have actually started to enjoy ourselves (or ceased being miserable), the next time the craving is slightly less potent as we are not coming at it from the point of view that we cannot imagine how we can cope without a drink, we are coming at it from the point of view that we can cope and even, for brief periods, actually enjoy ourselves. This makes the spiral of craving easier for us to short-circuit, so that on the next occasion there will be more situations that will act to short-circuit the spiral of craving, and the period of distraction will tend to be longer. This in turn builds up our confidence, and so the process will continue to improve. Also, as our physical and mental health improves, so does our feeling of well-being and confidence.

However, just as the process of developing a drinking problem can take many years, so the reversal can also take many years because what we are actually doing is reversing what the subconscious has learnt over many years: when under stress, reach for a drink. Every time the trigger comes and you don't take a drink, the subconscious is learning a new lesson: that alcohol is no longer available. The longer you have drunk for and the more deeply ingrained into your subconscious the triggers are, the longer it will take for the new lesson to be learnt. Fortunately, reversing the lessons learnt by the subconscious over many years can be greatly accelerated and, more importantly, the spiral of craving can be entirely avoided, if we approach it correctly. We will look at methods of doing this shortly, along with some other guidance designed to make stopping drinking as easy as possible. However, before we do this, there is one other psychological bar to stopping that we have not yet dealt with. It is closely linked with the spiral of craving in that it causes mental agony when we try to stop; however, it is a separate process and so needs to be considered separately. I refer to this as the Mental Agony of Stopping.

29.   The Mental Agony of Stopping

I ended up at the cinema the other day. My wife and I went with our two young boys, and watched a film called 'Trolls'.

For those unfamiliar with this film, let me give you an overview. The trolls are little creatures who are loving and happy, and spend their days dancing and hugging and generally loving life. The Bergens, however, are not like the trolls. They are bigger (big enough to pick up the trolls and eat them), and miserable. They don't hug, they don't sing, they don't dance. They are just miserable.

One day a miserable Bergan sees the trolls and sees how happy they are, and eats one, thinking it can then have the troll's happiness. And because it thinks it will be happy if it eats one, it is. Suddenly the whole race of Bergens becomes obsessed with eating trolls as they believe that the trolls are their sole source of happiness. The trolls run away, and the film is about the Bergens recapturing the trolls and the trolls trying to evade their fate of being eaten by the Bergens.

For those who have become sufficiently excited by my astounding storytelling ability to want to rush out and watch the film, stop reading now because I am about to tell you the ending. The trolls manage to convince the Bergens that it is ridiculous to think that you can eat something to make yourself happy, that there are many reasons to be happy; happiness comes from within and not from something you eat. So they all live happily ever after. This is very much a sign of the times, with the baddies being rehabilitated rather than defeated.

There is one particular scene in which the Bergen prince is sitting on his father the king's lap and is told by the king that he will never, ever be happy unless he eats trolls, and as the trolls have escaped he can never be happy. So the prince is miserable. He isn't miserable because he isn't eating trolls; he is miserable because the idea of being miserable your whole life is enough to make anyone miserable. He believes he will live a miserable life and it is that belief, not the lack of trolls to eat, that actually causes his unhappiness.

If you believe that you are going to spend the rest of your life unhappy, that belief alone will guarantee you will be miserable because the prospect of having a life of misery is a horrible one, enough to make anyone miserable. All you need is that genuine belief that you will be miserable. Of course we are never sat down on our father's laps and told, categorically and absolutely, that we will never be happy without alcohol (at least I hope that is true for most people). But of course we don't need to be, we have this belief instilled into us in a far more effective fashion. By society generally of course; through television programmes showing people drinking at every given opportunity; through friends, relatives, and colleagues serving drinks at every occasion; etc. But in fact, the main source of this belief comes from ourselves.

Every time you take a drink there is a little schizophrenic battle going on. On the one hand it is bad for you, it causes you x, y, and z problems, we are clearly better off without it, etc. And on the other hand? Well, the fact that we want it, of course. It gives us a short-term boost, and we want that boost. So we tell ourselves all kinds of excuses and lies to justify our decision to take the drink. The most recurrent of these excuses for most people is that a drink will make us happy (or happier, or less miserable, depending on where you are emotionally at the time). We force this view on ourselves again and again, so that when we come to stop we believe we won't be able to enjoy life, or certain situations, as much without a drink. Whether this is true or not is irrelevant. If you genuinely believe you now won't enjoy life, or even that you won't enjoy certain situations that you used to enjoy, that alone will be a cause of misery. This is reinforced by the fact that, as we have covered previously, the joy of socialising is often mistakenly chalked up as being due to drinking, and this in itself is reinforced by the fact that our own experience has shown us that we do not get this joy if we aren't drinking. We believe we will miss out on this joy when we stop, and this will cause us to be miserable. After all, we only get one life. Whether you believe in life after death, reincarnation, or oblivion, this is your only chance at this life, and if you believe that you are from here on missing out on a genuine pleasure then that life will be ever after spoiled to some degree, and this will be a cause of melancholy, sadness, and misery.

Now the misery isn't the end of it. An antidote for misery is hope. I have been through some fairly unpleasant situations during my lifetime, and the thing that kept me going through them is hope that things will get better. I remember reciting a section from a Levellers song to myself over and over again during my time in Iraq that goes '…there's never been a day that lasts forever, just as the sun sets, it will rise at dawn for ever after…'. It is a comfort sometimes, when there is no other, to remember that time moves inexorably on. Whatever misery or horror you are experiencing cannot last forever, things end, so there is always hope. But what if you are in a situation where you know that the misery can never end because it is self-inflicted and you have decided that the one thing you can do to alleviate your misery is the one thing that you can never allow yourself to do? After all we only get one life.

209

Whether you believe in life after death, reincarnation or oblivion this is your only chance at this life, and if you believe that you are from hereon missing out on a genuine pleasure then that life will be ever after spoiled to some degree, and this will be a cause of melancholy, sadness and misery. Well, then we move beyond misery and into misery with no hope of reprieve, and misery with no hope of reprieve is despair: utter, utter despair. This is the rock bottom for the addict, mentally if not physically. The drug is destroying them, mentally and physically; it is ruining their life, causing them to lose their job, their loved ones, their home, even their very life. But without it they have misery and despair. So often they tend to choose the drug. It may seem an irrational choice, but if you understand the mechanism properly is isn't. The misery of life with the drug is usually marginally better than the misery and despair the addict encounters when they try to give it up.

This not only explains why the addict will usually choose the drug over abstinence, but it also explains the tendency for them to jump from taking the drug, to abstinence, and back to taking the drug again. They are miserable with the drug, they know that logically they should be better off without it, so they stop, but then they encounter the misery and despair. So they start again, but they just end up back where they started with the misery of the drug, so they stop again. So the cycle continues. When you are unhappy you seek change. That is just human nature. The addict has only two choices: taking the drug or not taking it. These are the only two he or she can alternate between; there is no third way. Because both choices make them miserable, they are constantly flitting between the two.

This phenomenon also explains why the AA doctrine of taking one day at a time is so powerful. It's not so much that it breaks the recovery down into 'bitesize' pieces of single days, but more importantly, it can negate this phenomenon. The misery and despair evolves from contemplating our entire life without whatever substance it is that we believe we need to enjoy life (or to enjoy certain situations). However, if we are not thinking about our entire lives then we can short-circuit the entire process. The problem of course with this doctrine is that it doesn't solve the problem, it is just a way of ignoring it for a short period. After all, if we are determined to stop forever then we need to reconcile ourselves with that, not just ignore it every time the conflict arises.

This phenomenon also provides an explanation for why stopping for certain time-limited periods is often achievable, but stopping for good can be problematic. When we know that we will be starting drinking again at some point, again, we entirely negate this phenomenon. So just because you can stop short term, don't kid yourself into thinking that you are in control.

All in all it's a fairly bleak picture; either the misery of the drug or the misery of life without it. But there are two key points to note. Firstly, the entire process takes place in the conscious mind; therefore, it is within our power to control and negate it if we wish to do so. Secondly, the entire phenomenon is built on one key point: a genuine belief that you cannot be happy without drinking alcohol. And the beautiful truth is that this one single point from which the entire prison of addiction is built on is a lie, a fabrication. It is utterly wrong. You can enjoy life without alcohol; in fact, not only can you enjoy life without alcohol, but it is far more enjoyable. You just need to fully understand how the drug affects us and how every one of its perceived benefits is an illusion. With this in mind, let's now move on to consider a better way of stopping.

30.   A Better Way of Stopping – The Options

This book deals in detail with the intricacies of alcohol and alcohol addiction. However, any addiction, at its very simplest, is comprised of four main elements. There is usually (but not always) some kind of physical trigger (in the short term the physical withdrawal from the object of the addiction; in the long term, after the physical addiction has ceased, some kind of stress or anxiety or even simple hunger). This leads to the subconscious trigger, which in turn leads to the spiral of craving, and in the long term we encounter the mental agony of stopping. It is the spiral of craving and mental agony of stopping that causes the misery and despair that the addict faces when they are trying to give up the object of their addiction, and these two tend to be the most overpowering elements of any addiction.

Currently there are several methods of quitting any drug, but they all tend to focus on disrupting this four stage process in one way or another. Alternative drugs that are designed to ward off the withdrawal pangs tend to be the least effective. This is because the addiction doesn't fall down simply because there is no physical trigger. As noted previously, a spiral of craving can take place even without any physical trigger. If you want something you can't have you will be miserable, and if you sit there fantasising about it you will be even more miserable. Even with no physical trigger, that will be the case. It is also the case that these drugs used to disrupt the withdrawal have their own withdrawal, so in taking them you don't avoid the withdrawal but just delay it or drag it out even longer.

As discussed previously, Alcoholics Anonymous works by short-circuiting the spiral of addiction when it has already taken effect. The Allen Carr method works by stopping the craving from taking effect in the first place. For those of you who are not familiar with Allen Carr's various books on quitting, his method is essentially focused on demonstrating that there is no benefit to taking any particular drug and that the addict is better off without it. It is very effective for two reasons. Firstly, it prevents the subconscious triggers from leading to the spiral of craving. When the subconscious trigger kicks in, the result is not that the addict starts craving the drug; rather, they just act as a reminder of how lucky the addict is to be free. It actually turns the whole process on its head: the more triggers you get, the happier you are that you have stopped. In time the subconscious triggers themselves also tail off such that the addict ends up entirely free. Secondly, it entirely negates the mental agony of stopping. If the addict is genuinely glad to have stopped, and is looking forward to a life free from the drug, there is no expectation of misery and so no mental agony when stopping.

Essentially, any addiction exists because a part of the addict's mind misses the drug and the addict feels deprived and miserable when they stop taking it. If you can remove all the desire to take any particular drug then the addiction ceases to exist.

The Allen Carr method is an excellent system and it works very well for stopping smoking because Allen was a long-term heavy smoker and was therefore familiar with all the various intricacies of that particular addiction. However, it wasn't so effective for alcohol because he didn't cover any of the particular intricacies relating to alcohol, such as the physical withdrawal, the sleep deprivation, and the different time it takes for the mental relaxation to wear off compared with the physical intoxication, etc. It is essential that a complete and, above all, accurate picture of all the intricacies of each particular drug is fully understood for this method to be effective. After all, it is the addicts themselves that are best placed to judge whether what they are being told about any particular drug is correct or not, as it is they who are suffering each and every aspect of it. If they are being told that there is no plus side to any particular drug, this won't stop them because they know there is a plus side: every dose of their particular drug has given them a boost.

However, if you can explain the actual logical scientific reasons why a particular drug does not have a plus side because the perceived boost is actually only a reprieve from an unpleasant feeling caused by the particular drug in the first place, then you can properly convince them and thus disrupt the addiction process by both preventing the trigger from leading to a spiral of craving and negating the mental agony of stopping. On the other hand, if the information you are giving them about any particular drug is incorrect or incomplete they will sense this, on either a conscious or subconscious level, and the disruption won't take place effectively. They will continue to believe that their particular drug does have some benefit and that their life will be less enjoyable without it, and the addiction will continue.

Complete understanding is the key to the cure. With this in mind, let's now consider how best to go about stopping drinking.

Alcoholism, alcohol dependency, or problem drinking, whatever you want to call it, is essentially an interplay between the physical, the chemical, the physiological, and the psychological. All these factors that we have looked at in this book meld together to create confusion and the illusion of dependency. For those who have read and understood this book, the confusion and illusion will be gone, and so will the addiction. Indeed, for anyone, the only things standing between them and a life entirely free from alcohol are the subconscious triggers, the spiral of craving, and the mental agony of stopping; the effects of FAB; and finally (for those who are still drinking), the physical withdrawal. Let's now deal with these four hurdles in detail.

31. A Better Way of Stopping – The Subconscious Triggers, the Spiral of Craving, and the Mental Agony of Stopping

I am going to deal with these three aspects together as the method of countering them is identical. There is a conscious and subconscious knowledge that every drink does provide us with a boost. So even when we are through the physical withdrawal, whenever we feel stress or a need to relax there will be a part of us saying that we would like a drink. These triggers are going to hit us several times a day. It is like a dripping tap.

The main point to bear in mind is that the triggers simply create the thought of an alcoholic drink. It is what you do immediately after this thought enters your head that is key. If you allow this to start you off thinking about how nice it would be to have a drink, then before you know it you will be craving a drink. After all, even if you entirely remove the subconscious triggers, you are still going to be thinking about an alcoholic drink at various times for the rest of your life. To put it bluntly, there is alcohol in the world and you are going to encounter it, and this will start you off thinking about it. The best way to stop drinking is not to never think about alcohol; this is impossible. Nor is it to be constantly resisting the desire for a drink. The best way is to remove the desire. If we do this then it doesn't matter how many times we think about a drink, because if the desire to have a drink isn't there then there is no danger of our taking one. After all, no one forces you to take a drink apart from yourself, and if you do not want one you will not have one.

Let us turn again to the analogy of alcohol as a loan shark, a particularly spiteful and greedy one. This loan shark doesn't deal in money, however; it deals in feelings. It advances you good feelings, and you pay it back with bad feelings or unhappiness. And like any good loan shark, it will always, always take very much more than it gives.

Assume for the moment that human happiness is on a scale that runs from plus to minus 100. So plus 100 is the happiest we can ever be, and minus 100 is the most unhappy we can be. When you have a drink you get a plus-five boost. But as the effect wears off and the body counters the effect of the alcohol, we then encounter a minus ten. So overall we are worse off. The only way we can take the drink and not have the minus ten is to take another drink, and another, and another. Even then we will eventually have the bad feelings, most probably when we are asleep or unconscious, in which case our sleep will be unrestful and we will wake up feeling more tired than we did the night before.

Also bear in mind that this is only the physical side. As soon as you take that drink there will be many, many other points lost as a result of other matters. When you stop drinking there is a great sense of achievement, but as soon as you take a drink there is a feeling of despair and failure. If you are a problem drinker with people relying on you to stop, this will be all the more exacerbated as their disappointment and misery become apparent.

So when the thought of a drink enters your head, don't leave it to fester; counteract it. Make an effort to see it realistically. When we stop, we often fantasise about drinking. But fantasising is exactly that: it is a fantasy. A fantasy is something that we imagine where we cut out all the bad parts that would, in reality, be part and parcel of the whole process. Don't allow yourself to fantasise about it, see it as it really is. Don't just think of how nice it would be to drink one drink, think of the whole picture. Think of the unpleasant feeling as the drink wears off (if you are intending to have only one drink) or the start of the whole miserable cycle. If you are realistic, you will see that if you start again you will very quickly spiral back to your old drinking habits and even beyond. Imagine the feeling of failure, of letting down those relying on you. Think of waking up in the night and lying there worrying, of getting up the next day feeling exhausted and depressed. Don't just let the thought of having a drink float there unattended: pin it down and be realistic, see the whole picture and not just part of it.

By doing this we are forcing a new lesson on our conscious and subconscious alike. Although the subconscious learns from repetition over time, the greater the impact, the quicker the lesson will be learnt. The effect of one alcoholic drink is small and it makes little impact on our subconscious; consequently, it takes many years and thousands of drinks before the subconscious learns the lessons that create the addiction.

However, if the effect is great then the subconscious learns the lesson that much quicker. Have you ever reached into an oven and touched the heating element? I did so recently, when our oven was broken and I was trying to fix it. The electricity supply to the oven was off and the oven was clearly stone cold, but my subconscious mind was screaming at me not to touch it. I knew, for an absolute fact, that the element was cold, but I couldn't resist giving it a very quick tap to make sure it was cold before I grasped it firmly. I don't recall ever having been burnt by an oven heating element, and I don't even remember looking at one in the oven while it was on. If I have, I have only done it once or twice in my entire life. However, because the effect of being very badly burnt is so great, my subconscious has learnt the lesson after very few repetitions, maybe even as few as one.

So although it can take years for the subconscious triggers to become fully imbedded, they can be reversed in a fraction of the time if, every time you receive a trigger, you stop, and you counter it as fully and as thoroughly as you can, taking as long as you need to. Don't just let it float by: take the opportunity to force the lesson on your subconscious, to make a large impact on the subconscious and thus make the process of reversing the subconscious triggers even quicker.

You won't be able to do this all the time, as life sometimes dictates its own pace. If you are rushing through a supermarket in a hurry and get a trigger when you pass the wine aisle, or if you are at an important business lunch and get a pang when the drinks are ordered, you won't be able to take some time alone to counter the triggers. However, do as much as you can. If you don't drink, the triggers won't get any worse, and every time you fully counter one they will diminish, so do as much as you can as soon as you can. It is impossible to give any firm time frame, but if you do it properly you can have broken the back of it within around three weeks. Like most things in life, making effort at the start actually means we have to make less effort overall.

The other point to mention is that you can actually start this process before you stop drinking. If you are still drinking, start analysing every part of your drinking. Think about the taste, the effect the first drink has, then the second, etc. Stop when you are drinking and see how you actually feel. Is the feeling of being drunk or the feeling of having a drink or two inside you so fantastic? What's so good about it? If you actually stop and think about it, the feeling alcohol gives us is just a slightly numb feeling, the main benefit of which is to numb the myriad of unpleasant feelings that it has caused in the first place. Is it really something you want to squander your money, your health, your friends and family, your self-respect, even your very life on? Analyse also very closely the feeling when the drink wears off: how you feel when you wake up, either lying awake in the night worrying, riddled with despair and self-loathing, or getting up in the morning feeling depressed and tired? Think of that loan shark: is what you are obtaining worth what you ultimately have to repay?

Bear in mind also that the relaxing feeling that the first drink of the day creates is simply the removal of a feeling of anxiety and tiredness that has been entirely created by all the previous alcoholic drinks you have consumed. Remember also that even if there is genuine stress that is seemingly relieved by taking a drink, the relief won't remove the cause of the stress. That will still be there the next day, and the poisoning effect of the alcohol coupled with the lack of restful sleep will mean you will be less able to cope with it the following day, are more likely to be stressed from it, and are even more likely to need a drink the following day.

If you are countering the triggers effectively (and even if you are really busy, you should have time to at least remind yourself you are far better off without drinking and any pleasure was a clever illusion), then you will not get cravings. A trigger only leads to the spiral of craving if the trigger causes you to start thinking about how nice it would be to have a drink and about the possibility of having one. If you have a trigger and know full well you don't want a drink and won't have one, then even if you take no steps to counter the trigger then the spiral of craving won't start. Indeed, if your mindset is correct then even the subconscious triggers won't be a problem, they will just put the thought of an alcoholic drink into your mind. If your mindset is such that you are only too happy to be free from the whole filthy mess, then every subconscious trigger will be the opportunity to remind yourself how lucky you are that you now have the knowledge to free yourself. The spiral of craving only starts if you entertain the possibility, however remote, of taking a drink. As soon as you do that you are thinking about the reality of having a drink, how it will taste, the effect, etc. You won't

224

be able to think about anything else, and soon the spiral will be in full sway.

So in a perfect world you won't have any craving. But we don't live in a perfect world, so let's deal with what you should do if you do start craving.

Running through the thought process on subconscious triggers detailed above will work. Indeed, reminding yourself of the grim reality of drinking will not only reverse the subconscious triggers, it will also prevent a spiral of craving from taking effect. You will stop craving something if you convince yourself it is repulsive and dreadful and has no benefit at all. If you have to, take yourself out of the situation you are in. No matter what situation you are in you should be able to pop to the toilet for a few minutes just to be alone. If it is really bad, just leave. You will form your own opinion of whether stopping drinking takes priority over whatever it is you are doing.

However, I emphasise that if you fully understand the contents of this book you will have no reason to crave, and there will be no mental agony when stopping. You will receive triggers, but they will not evolve into the full craving, and a contemplation of a life free from alcohol will be a cause of happiness, not misery. If this is not

225

the case then you have missed the point somewhere along the way and a part of you still retains some belief that there is some genuine benefit to drinking alcohol. Try to pin down why you believe alcohol has any benefit, then analyse and exorcise this belief. It usually helps if you can speak to someone about it (at the end of the book I provide details of the website for this book, through which I can be contacted, and I will always respond to any queries if I can). There are also two other things you can do to make it even more unlikely that a full spiral of craving will take effect.

The first one is certainty. The spiral only starts if the possibility of having a drink enters your mind. If there is no possibility of your having a drink, if there is absolute certainty that you will never have another, there can be no spirals. So you need to make a solemn vow that you will never ever take another drink, whatever happens. You may have made and broken such a vow previously on occasions too numerous to mention. However, you need to know that this time is different. Previously you did not have the requisite knowledge to defeat your adversary. Now you do, so nothing can prevent your victory. In fact, it is not victory that looks impossible, but failure. How can you fail to stop taking something that you have absolutely no desire to take? The key to defeating addiction is not overcoming a desire for something; it is removing that desire in its entirety.

The other thing to think about is that people usually only consider drinking again in the belief that this time they can control it and drink within certain predefined parameters. Indeed, you may be someone who has only ever drunk within certain predefined parameters, someone who could not be considered to have a drink problem in any way, shape, or form. You need to remind yourself that drinking sensibly cannot last, that the natural tendency is to drink more and more, not less and less. For those who have a serious drinking problem, you need to remind yourself that if you do take a drink, even one, you will precipitate right back to where you were when you stopped. No one would take a drink if they knew that in doing so they would have to drink all day every day for the rest of their very short lives, sacrificing their friends, family, home, job, self-respect, and their very life. If you get this fact straight in your mind, if you know that it has to be all or nothing, you won't get cravings because you will know that having just one drink, or drinking within certain predefined parameters, is impossible. If you have any doubts on this, reread the chapter on 'Just One Drink'.

32.   A Better Way of Stopping – The Effects of FAB

By understanding how FAB works you are already a substantial way towards negating its effect. If I look through a magnifying glass at an ant I don't jump out of my skin because I have seen a giant ant, I know how the magnifying glass works and know that the ant isn't giant, it just appears so because of the illusion created by the glass. In the same way, when you start to think fondly of alcohol and your drinking years you will know that this is the effect of FAB and that your memory of events has become warped over time. However, even when you realise this, the thoughts can be compelling and hard to dismiss. So it will help if we do more than just recognise and expect it.

It was never the initial stopping that was the problem for me, as being a binge drinker I went through the physical withdrawal regularly. The problem I had was staying stopped. Often, when we reach the stage when we are actually going to make an attempt to stop, we are utterly sick of the whole thing. We are living with the reality of it and it is grim and we are only too glad to stop.

The real issue is when FAB starts to kick in, when the grim reality is left behind and we end up with some happy fantasy of what it was like to drink. If you are still drinking now or have recently stopped, one method that can be very effective to counter the effects of FAB is to use the human happiness scale I mentioned previously that runs from plus to minus 100, with 100 being the happiest we can ever be and minus 100 the most unhappy we can be. While you are still drinking, commit key parts of your day to paper. When you wake up, make a quick note of the circumstances (e.g. 'drank heavily the night before', or 'had a fair amount the night before' etc.) and note down roughly where you think you are on the scale. Do it after your first drink of the day, after the first bout, whatever. Do it as often as you can, maybe even hourly, and note down any particularly bad points (such as an argument while you had been drinking, losing your temper, feeling depressed or miserable for any reason). The one thing I would say is try not to let it be influenced by your upcoming cessation. If you are having a bad time due, directly or indirectly, to your drinking, it will seem a lot less awful if you are confident that you are about to stop. That plus shouldn't factor. What you are looking to produce is an accurate account of your life as a drinker, not an account of your life as a drinker who is feeling happier because they are about to stop.

When you do make an entry, try to take a few moments to do it in peace and in private. You need to stop and consider the whole. Not just how you actually feel, but your life generally. So the time of the first drink of the day would usually be a high point for most people.

229

When you are riding on that particular crest, stop and analyse it properly. Are you really genuinely happy, or have you just anaesthetised that unpleasant feeling caused by your previous drinking? Analyse fully how you feel. Don't put your other problems out of your mind as they have not gone away; mark in relation to the whole.

If you do genuinely believe that you are happy from that first drink, then give it half an hour and mark again. How do you score after one hour, then three, then four? Are you still riding the wave of elevation? Or are you just now so drunk that you don't really know how you feel? If you are marking honestly you will find that the initial good feeling is not the ecstasy you believe it to be and it is very short lived. Any good feeling quickly disseminates even when you continue to drink, and you are left feeling dulled and miserable. All in all, you will find life generally is not pleasant, and the small highs are far outweighed by the numerous and substantial lows. Is the short high worth the long low when you come to in the morning, or during the night? Where exactly do you come on the happiness scale then?

Feel free to write down as much detail as you can, as the point is to record in writing the reality of your life as a drinker.

When you stop drinking, try to keep the marking system going for a bit. If you are feeling rotten then are you within the first few days of stopping? If so then you may well feel rotten for a bit, but you just have to wait it out. This stage will soon be gone, never to return. After two or three days you will really be on the up. When you mark now, always bear in mind that you have stopped drinking, you have solved the main problem in your life. Even aside from this, you will find you are marking much higher overall as your physical and mental health returns.

If you do have a day or occasion that is particularly bad or awful then mark it down for what it is, but also imagine how different things would be if you were still drinking. Then you would not only have whatever it is that has caused you to be miserable, but also all the downsides of drinking in addition to that. Think of the loan shark. However awful you feel, if you drink, you are not removing the problem, you are just anaesthetising it slightly, and moreover you will pay for that temporary relief a dozen times over.

What this diary will really do is to counteract the effect of FAB; however, it is also an excellent exercise to help counter the subconscious triggers and ensure the craving does not take a hold. It will cement the reality of drinking in written form. If ever you start to look at your drinking years through rose tinted spectacles, you will have the reality in written form to refer to.

33. A Better Way of Stopping – Undermining the Addiction

As mentioned previously, the key to defeating addiction is to explode the myth that there is any benefit or pleasure in whatever drug the addict is seeking to quit. So is there really any pleasure in drinking? Let's use what we have learnt so far to see if we can't answer this question once and for all. Let's now turn our minds to this supposed pleasure of drinking.

Let's make it really difficult for ourselves and take an absolutely top of the range drinking occasion. I can't tell you what yours are, but I can tell you what a few of mine were up until a few years ago. It would be the end of a day, the end of a difficult working day. But a difficult day where I got things done and got results, where I left the office with everything that needed doing done. I would be tired but pleased. It would also be a day where there was a lot of running around, so I would be physically tired as well. It would be an early evening, an early Friday evening, at the start of a long weekend or even a holiday. In fact it would be a long hard day at work, then travelling on holiday with all the physical exertion of lugging the whole family's suitcases around, unpacking, then finally sitting down in the warm evening, on a balcony overlooking the sea, freshly showered and dressed, drinking an ice-cold bottle of beer.

Or it would be Christmas, coming into a warm house from the freezing cold and having a nice hot glass of mulled wine, heavily laced with brandy.

Or going to a fine restaurant, with a view of the City of London stretching out below me, and sipping that dark, rich glass of red wine.

Thoughts like these can be compelling; they can scupper an attempt to stop before it even gets started. We can be months away from our next holiday, Christmas, or meal out. In fact, these are almost exclusively situations which are so idyllic that they will never exist anyway. But their power lies in the fact that they show to us that our lives will never be the same without a drink, that this one life we have been granted is now tinged forever due to the absence of alcohol.

So is it possible to rob these compelling, overpowering thoughts of their power? To prove to your own satisfaction that there is no pleasure in drinking? The answer, you will be pleased to hear, is yes. I cannot do it for you, you have to do it for yourself, but I can describe how I went about it.

Let's start with the holiday example. It can be broken down into the following:

1. The end of a difficult working day.

2. Satisfaction of a hard day's work well done.

3. Rest when physically and mentally tired.

4. An early Friday evening at the start of a long weekend or even a holiday.

5. Starting a holiday when all the physical exertion of lugging the whole family's suitcases around and unpacking them is done.

6. Sitting down on a warm evening on a balcony overlooking the sea.

7. Freshly showered.

8. Dressed in nice holiday clothes.

9. Drinking an ice-cold bottle of beer.

I suppose you could break it down even further, but let's keep it to these nine for now.

The key point here is that eight of those nine items are enjoyable in and of themselves. They are not reliant on alcohol to be enjoyable. Even the ninth one is only partially reliant on alcohol. Drinking an ice-cold drink when you are thirsty is an immense pleasure, but it could be water, juice, soda, or an alcohol free beer. So the only thing you get from the alcohol would be a slightly dulled feeling. When you analyse it you can see that alcohol gets the credit for this perfect evening, but actually it's contributed nothing to it at all. In fact it has detracted from it. In the very best case, that one drink will disturb your sleep so that you are tired and out of sorts for the first day of your holiday. In fact, it is much more realistic that you won't just stop at one drink, and the more drinks you have the more chance you have of marring that otherwise idyllic situation with a drunken argument, an actual hangover, and a feeling of self-loathing the next day.

With the Christmas example, coming into a warm place when you are cold is always a pleasure, as is a hot drink, the smell of Christmas, a decorated house, the great day ahead. Again, what would alcohol add, other than a slightly dulled feeling and a risk (if not a certainty) of much greater misery. I have had Christmases drinking and Christmases sober. The drinking ones ended in blackouts and arguments that I could not remember. The sober ones were genuinely enjoyable.

The same goes for the meal in the restaurant. What would alcohol add other than a slightly dulled feeling and the promise of misery to come?

Alcohol takes too much credit. It takes credit for situations that it has contributed nothing too, or has even actually detracted from.

As I say, I cannot rob your compelling thoughts of their power, but you can, by going through the process that I have just gone through above. You have to go through this process with all your drinking situations – not just the really idyllic ones, but all of them. Think of every time you might be tempted to drink and go through the process. Think of the barbeque, the holiday, coming home after a day at work, passing the bar or supermarket, having a meal, meeting friends, having an argument with your spouse or partner, losing a loved one, going on a business trip, or having a meal out. Don't wait until you find yourself in these situations and just hope that you won't drink, and don't avoid them altogether. Prepare yourself before you even get there. See now how you will cope with, or enjoy them, without a drink. In fact, see and understand how you will cope with them that much better, and enjoy them that much more, without alcohol. As a human being you have the benefit of imagination. Imagine yourself in these various situations, and imagine yourself enjoying them all the more without alcohol –

without the intoxication and all the downsides associated with it – enjoying them safe in the knowledge that you will not lose control, that you will not have a drunken argument, that you will not have a broken and restless night, that you will not wake up full of self-loathing and worry and exhaustion and misery.

It takes time. And it takes effort. But it is achievable. And the reward is no less than the end of the addiction.

34.   A Better Way of Stopping – The Physical Withdrawal

As stated previously, if you are going to stop drinking you should consult your doctor or physician to see if you need monitoring during the physical withdrawal stage. Most people will not. The process I have detailed above in the chapter on stopping cold turkey deals with the physical withdrawal. It consists of one bad day, two at the outside, then two or three days when you are under par but well over the worst. And this is in the worst case for the heaviest drinkers; most people will have an easier time of it, and many will just have one bad day.

Whichever category you fall into, there is no easy way round it: you just have to be prepared to suffer for a day or two. Pass the time as best you can, and if you can concentrate on a book or the telly, do so, If you are really twitched up, however, you won't be able to. Just eat and drink when you can, and if you possibly can, go for a walk. Any exercise will help, not only to pass the time but also to give you the best chance of getting some sleep.

The first night is the worst: lying wide awake, nervous and miserable, watching the clock and watching every second of the night tick past is not the best way to spend a night. If you manage to get any sleep at all you are doing better than I did! All you can do is remind yourself that this feeling will soon be gone, never to return, and that this first night is the worst you will suffer. There are chat rooms on the internet for alcoholics and problem drinkers. Due to the nature of alcoholism and the fact that they are used by people from all over the world with their own different time zones, there are always people online to talk to. This can be a good way of passing the time. Just be aware that people who have not read and understood this book may give you incorrect advice on stopping. They do so with the best intentions, but if it contradicts the advice or information in this book ignore it, and never ever doubt your decision. It will also help you to get through this stage if you keep in mind the very real benefits you are about to gain.

35.　The Benefits of Stopping

By far the greatest benefit of stopping drinking is to get back to your peak physical and mental health. People simply do not appreciate how much our mental resilience is tied to our physical health. Hangovers, lack of sleep, and the physical degradation generally leave us feeling unable to cope with life. After only a few days of stopping, your quality of life improves dramatically, and it continues to improve for some time.

Another major benefit is to take control of your life again, to regain the lost self-respect, to know that you have solved the biggest problem in your life. Very quickly your physical and mental well-being returns, leaving you mentally and physically stronger and better equipped to deal with the stresses and strains of life generally. This alone makes stopping well worthwhile. As your physical and mental health return, you will feel better than you ever did when you were drinking. But there are numerous other benefits of stopping that all add up.

No drinker fully appreciates the effect their drinking has on other people. A drinker suffers continually from sleep deprivation and an anxious, worried feeling. How easy do you think it would be to deal with, or live with, someone who is constantly anxious and tired?

241

Such people are snappy and unpleasant. The person can't see it themselves, they just find everything annoying and are constantly getting into arguments and bickering. They think it is because the people they are dealing with are irritating, and they simply cannot see that it is they and not the other parties that are causing the problem. One of the extraordinary things I found when I stopped drinking was that I was not the impatient, intolerant person I thought I was, and that the world simply isn't the irritating place I thought it was. This alone has had a hugely positive impact on my personal relationships and quality of life generally.

If the drinker isn't suffering the withdrawal of alcohol which causes them to be irritable, they are drinking, which is even worse. Drunk people are irritating when you are sober, there is no getting around that. And when I say drunk I don't just mean falling down drunk; even people who have only had a couple of drinks can be irritating when you are sober. Also bear in mind that emotions run unchecked when we drink. When the drinker is drinking they tend to become angry, introspective, tearful, etc. Either way, they are an unpleasant person to be around. Again, they can't see it and tend to blame it on the world around them rather than themselves. Stopping sets everything back to where it ought to be, and it lets you be the best person you can without any effort, it just happens naturally. It is amazing to find that so many problems you see with other people or the world just don't exist when you are back on an even keel. The WC Fields/Charlie Harper portrayals of the alcoholic are false, they are pure fiction. In reality they would not be the happy-go-lucky people we see on screen. They would be bad tempered, argumentative, and unhappy.

Heavy drinkers whose hair is going grey often find that within a couple of months of stopping their hair stops turning grey, and may even return to some extent to its previous colour. I found this myself. You will also very likely lose weight and find that your appetite changes. I myself found that I naturally wanted healthier food and had less craving for fast, highly calorific food.

Another of the considerable advantages is the improved quality of life as your broken sleeping patterns repair and you begin to catch up on the lost sleep. This will have a phenomenal impact on your quality of life. Waking up feeling fresh and ready to go is one of the great feelings in life.

Another aspect of life you will enjoy more if you go about stopping in the right way is social situations. I have always struggled in social situations and this is one of the reasons I drank in the first place. Now, in a social situation where alcohol is being served, I always feel one up whether lots of drink is being consumed or not. If people are drinking a lot and getting drunk I feel pleased not to be a part of that anymore because, to put it frankly, drunk people are phenomenally irritating when you are sober. They repeat themselves, they talk too loudly, they get too close to you, they say stupid things. Drink really seems to bring out people's pettiness and ignorance. It is an absolute pleasure not to be a part of that anymore, and to know that, unlike the drinkers, I will be waking up refreshed and happy instead of anxious, hung over, and exhausted. On the other hand, if there is alcohol but everyone is drinking very moderately I'm even more relieved, as I'm left thinking 'thank God I'm not still drinking or I'd be the only one here drunk', or else 'thank God I'm not still drinking or I'd be stood here with an empty glass craving another because the drinks just aren't coming quick enough!'

Ultimately, what it comes down to is a vastly improved quality of life.

36.   Conclusions

Let's take a moment here to summarise the main points.

1.   Alcohol is an anaesthetic and a depressant. The human brain
      reacts to it as such by releasing stimulants to counter the
      depressant effects of the alcohol. Every time we take a drink
      the brain becomes more efficient at doing this, with the result
      that over time the insecure, unpleasant after-effect of drinking
      becomes more pronounced and surfaces quicker and quicker
      as our drinking years wear on. However, because alcohol is a
      depressant and ultimately sends us to sleep, we tend to drink
      towards the end of the day and hence sleep through the worst
      of the withdrawal. But we do not entirely escape the ill effects
      of the withdrawal, as it impacts our quality of sleep and
      remnants of it persist into the following day.

2.   Addiction takes hold in the subconscious. Because alcohol is
      drunk (rather than, for example, being injected or snorted)
      there is a significant (in terms of addiction at least) time lapse
      between the drinking of the drink and the relaxing effect. It
      can take some time, therefore, for the subconscious to link the
      two together, so it can take some years of drinking before
      addiction to alcohol starts to take a hold.

3.   The period of addiction to alcohol is lengthened even further because when we start drinking we know, on a conscious and subconscious level, that the ill effects of drinking can be remedied by abstinence, so when we have any adverse effects from drinking we are turned off alcohol. They very thought of it makes us feel physically sick. It takes some years before we categorically learn, on both a conscious and a subconscious level, that the ill effects of drinking can be remedied by more drinking. In effect, what happens is that we contaminate our subconscious mind with the knowledge that the ill effects of drinking can be alleviated (in the short term at least) with more drinking. The subconscious adapts to this, and over time our reaction when faced with the ill effects of drinking is to want more drink to alleviate the ill effects, rather than to be repulsed by alcohol until we have recovered.

4.   The subconscious triggers set off the spiral of craving, which creates an absolute obsession with the object of our craving. The spiral of craving is an extremely powerful force and is much more powerful than the subconscious triggers. However, unlike the subconscious triggers, it takes place

entirely in our conscious mind and as such it is entirely our decision whether to crave or not.

5. The physical impairment or intoxication does not dissipate at the same time as the feeling of mental relaxation. The mental relaxation always dissipates quicker, so to maintain a certain constant level of relaxation and contentment we have to become increasingly intoxicated. This disparity increases as our drinking years wear on and our bodies become more and more proficient at countering the anaesthetising effects of the alcohol.

6. The actual feeling of being under the influence of alcohol is nothing, it is just a slightly dulled feeling. Alcohol only confers an actual (apparent) benefit when we have an unpleasant feeling to anaesthetise. The vast majority of these unpleasant feelings are in fact caused by our previous drinking in the first place

7. Even when we are suffering from an unpleasant or negative emotion that is not caused by our previous drinking, a drink will often end up exaggerating this feeling. The mental relaxation quickly wears off and needs to be replaced, and the increasing physical intoxication that results from the

additional drinks depresses the regulator in our brain that prevents our emotions from running away with us. The result is that we end up suffering more from the negative emotion even when we are drinking, to say nothing of the following day's hangover. Before we know it, we are waking up feeling dreadful and depressed and a hundred times worse than we did with the original stress that caused us to drink in the first place.

8.   If you are happy and relaxed at social occasions, your brain will release certain chemicals that can make you feel euphoric. As we often start out drinking at social occasions it is the alcohol that is usually mistakenly credited with this feeling. This is reinforced as we tend not the get the feeling if we aren't drinking; however, this is actually caused by the fact that usually when we aren't drinking we feel uncomfortable and are therefore not relaxed.

9.   Addiction to alcohol essentially occurs when the brain realises, on both a conscious and subconscious level, that the ill effects of the previous drinking can be remedied by more drinking. This lesson can never be unlearnt. Stopping drinking, no matter how long for, can never reverse this knowledge. The mental associations that make up

'alcoholism' can never be unlearnt. If you get to the stage that you instinctively know that the unpleasant feeling created by one alcoholic drink can be relieved by another drink, then you can never drink safely again. Whether you have stopped for a week, a month, a year, or 50 years, the mental associations will remain.

10. Alcohol ruins sleep. Even one alcoholic drink will interrupt the natural sleeping pattern.

11. Alcohol does not taste good. Any human being is naturally repulsed by it.

12. Our view of our own drinking changes over time. The further we are from our last drink, the more fondly and benignly we think of our drinking years. The actual reality fades and we are left with some happy fantasy of what our drinking years were like.

13. The mental agony of stopping is based entirely on the belief that life will be less enjoyable without drinking, which is in itself based on the belief that there is genuine pleasure in drinking. Fortunately, these beliefs are entirely incorrect. If you believe the truth, which is that life is far more enjoyable

without drinking, then you can entirely negate this mental agony and remove the addiction.

14.   While the disease theory of alcoholism does provide some safety by preventing (some) alcoholics from ever drinking again, it allows far too many people to fall into the trap in the first place. When people start drinking they find they can control it and can stop when they want to; therefore, they think they are clearly not an alcoholic and can drink with impunity. The tendency, therefore, is to drink irresponsibly in the erroneous belief that they are safe.

15.   The unpleasant, insecure feeling created by one drink is similar to the usual stresses and strains we encounter in life, such that the subconscious will not differentiate between the two. Therefore, however long an alcoholic has stopped drinking for, they can still have cravings for a drink every time they encounter any stress in their lives.

16.   Alcoholism is not a genetic condition. Anyone can become an alcoholic, it just takes a few years of drinking, and if you drink heavily or irresponsibly then the process takes place that much quicker.

17.   Alcohol withdrawal in a significant and noticeable form is much more prevalent that people think. Many people admit to having disturbed sleep and night worries after drinking. This is quite simply the withdrawal effects from alcohol. They may not have any temptation to relieve these by having a drink, but they are suffering from them.

In fact, the main question we really need to ask is why do we drink? Are we getting more out of it than we are putting in? In fact, are we actually getting anything out of it at all? If the answer is 'no' then the obvious conclusion is to stop. The problem is that the feeling of insecurity and anxiety caused by drinking occurs some time after the drink has been consumed, and in fact the immediate after-effect of taking a drink is for that feeling to recede slightly. Every time we take a drink, therefore, we associate it with a temporary removal of that insecure, anxious feeling and we are fooled into thinking that the drink is actually a friend rather than an enemy. In fact, every single drink you take in your life enforces the erroneous lesson in both your conscious and subconscious mind, so that over a matter of days, weeks, months, and years you become increasingly reliant on alcohol. You become increasingly inclined to drink more rather than less, and every time you have any stress or unhappiness in your life you think that a drink will help, that it will remove that empty, insecure feeling. And the fact is that it will. But only temporarily. Then that feeling will return, only stronger than before, and the only thing that will get rid of it is another drink, or increasingly stronger drugs. This is why drug addiction is also associated with alcohol consumption. Many people realise when they are drinking (either consciously or subconsciously) that the drink is simply not doing what it should, as the body becomes increasingly adept at counteracting the alcohol with stimulants. That, coupled with alcohol's tendency to remove our fear and make us act recklessly, makes us more inclined to move onto harder drugs. The question we ought to be asking ourselves is not 'do I have a problem and so need to stop?' but 'am I getting more out of this than I am putting in?' – the answer to this latter question is no!

If you found this book useful then please help others to benefit from it by spreading the word. Please take the time to leave a review on Amazon, which is this book's main marketing platform. Every single review can make a huge difference. Also the website (www.alcoholexplained.com) contains a PDF of the first five chapters of the book, which can be read for free. Please send the link to these chapters to anyone you think may find this book useful or interesting. They may find, as I am hoping many of you will, that this book has a dramatic and very positive influence on their lives and will help explain, simply and conclusively, what was previously thought to be inexplicable. My main hope for this book is that it will benefit people, and people can only benefit from it if they are aware of it. Please take the time to tell people about it and talk about it. In addition, if you would like to provide any comments or feedback, or if you have any questions, I would be very glad to hear from you. These can be sent via the website.

Also by William Porter:

Alcohol Explained 2

Covering some topics covered in the original Alcohol Explained more detail, but also covering several entirely new topics, with an emphasis on tools you can use to get you, and keep you, sober.

"William nails it again in his second book on alcohol. Reading both books has honestly changed the way I think about this socially acceptable drug. I am now 9 months sober and never looking back! Thank you for giving me the tools I needed to get my life back!"

Amazon Review

Diet and Fitness Explained

Ever wished you could eat whatever fast food you liked, take no exercise, and be slim and healthy? Well you can't. But you can do the next best thing, which is to enjoy healthy food even more than you enjoy fast food, and enjoy exercising even more than you enjoy sitting on the sofa. Diet and Fitness Explained is the book that gets under the skin of our eating habits, and provides a simple, easy to understand guide to the entire riddle of diet and fitness.

"I read Alcohol explained by William Porter and it changed my life. I then read this book and although I love fitness and health, it explained things differently. So easy to digest (excuse the pun) and absorb. The writing suits me perfectly. All information is superbly presented. I would recommend anyone who wants to become healthier, or even to challenge their present views on food etc to purchase this book."

Amazon Review

Nicotine Explained

Want to understand your smoking / vaping habits? Feel like you should quit but enjoy it too much? Nicotine Explained is the book that gets under the skin of our smoking and vaping habits and explains what nicotine does for us, what it doesn't do for us, and how it becomes an indispensable part of our lives. This is the understanding you need to regain control of your life.

"Brought me, and my smoking to a standstill...I'm still absorbing the huge amount this little book has to offer, and I will always refer to it. This is the education I hoped for."

Amazon Review

The Alcohol Explained Workbook

This is the workbook to accompany and to be used in conjunction with the book Alcohol Explained. This workbook offers a step-by-step approach to breaking down alcohol and drinking, allowing the reader to turn the reading of the book into a more immersive,

learning experience.